ROMANCING THE DIVINE

A STORY ABOUT TRUE LOVE

DON NORI

Destiny Image Fiction

An Imprint of

Destiny Image® Publishers, Inc.
P.O. Box 310
Shippensburg, PA 17257-0310

ISBN 0-7684-2053-9

For Worldwide Distribution

Printed in the U.S.A.

This book and all other Destiny Image, Revival Press, MercyPlace, Fresh Bread, Destiny Image Fiction, and Treasure House books are available at Christian bookstores and distributors worldwide.

For a U.S. bookstore nearest you, call **1-800-722-6774**.
For more information on foreign distributors, call **717-532-3040**.
Or reach us on the Internet:

www.destinyimage.com

Contents

True Love

How noble true love is! How invincible! How pure! How innocent!

Love simply comes, often undetected even by the one overtaken by its mysterious powers.

True love. The lonely covet its reality. The arrogant flaunt its presence. The ignorant snub its wonder.

It is as illogical as anything can be. It is hopeless to describe it and folly to shun it.

The greatest philosophers have sought to define it. Religion has tried to buy it. Many have tried to elude it.

Love is as hopeless to understand as it is impossible to deny. Yet reason and logic are helpless against love, for it is a most formidable foe of the mundane and the average. True love, you see, dares to go places where reason cannot tread. Love sees realities about which philosophy can only hope to dimly speculate.

True love knows what tradition can only distantly remember.

True love draws the least lovable. It can make anyone a hero.

True love is the sustaining power of the universe itself, yet is so lovely that it abides fully in the hearts of those foolish enough to respond to its rapturous invitation to come.

The Peril of True Love

*L*ove without legalism; commitment without control; fullness without fear; relationship without religion—the very mention of such possibilities brings feelings of exhilaration and hope, for they are the deepest yearnings of our souls.

They are the essence of true love.

But these passions of the heart are so foreign to the sacred teachings we have been taught, that to risk harboring such intimate thoughts borders upon heresy.

Yet that is the peril of true love.

That is the inevitable price of desire.

Love will cause one to take risks that make a normal person shudder, as though true love is not for the commoner. But when one has fallen hopelessly, desperately, eternally in love, nothing is predictable, nothing is ordinary about this love. In fact, it turns the average person into a hopelessly lovesick and desperate human being. It transforms the way he thinks, the things he does, and the way he prays. True love changes his view of life and determines his reason for living.

The invasion of true love into the heart of any human being turns that person into someone quite extraordinary indeed. For nothing...*nothing* will ever be the same again. Nothing else will satisfy as it once satisfied, nothing else will ever be worth living for.

Predictably, true love will always have its detractors. "Are you crazy?" is the inevitable question from these who have either never experienced true love or who have forgotten its illogical and all-consuming captivity. And just like everyone else who has ever been moonstruck by this...this unexplainable, undeniable supernatural force, you respond with a wistful, faraway look in your eyes, "Yes. If by finding true love you mean crazy, then, yes, I believe I am."

"But don't you realize what this means?" the grilling continues. "Don't you understand what an uproar this will cause? People will think you have gone off the deep end for sure. They will say, you have gone into heresy. People will write about you in their books!"

"If true love is heresy, then I am happy to be in heresy," you respond with unmistakable resolve in your voice. "True love is worth the ridicule of man. If I am to be accused of anything so heinous, let it be for this love. May the accusation be that I fell in love, and that love consumed me, and drove me to pay any price for it.

"But I can see why some would wonder. True love has that effect on a person. It happened to me. It drove me to abandon all that I ever was, as if I have ever been anyone of importance. It drove me to ignore the limited boundaries of mere mortal man and joyfully pursue Him whom my soul loves."

You see, love makes God real.

True love destroys the way religion has told us faith is supposed to be. Love ignores her critics and yields to the sweet comfort of desire deep within the human heart.

True love never ends and can never be destroyed. True love cannot be reasoned with, nor can it be reasoned away, for it has little to do with the intellect but it has everything to do with that which the intellect can never touch. True love dwells so much higher than understanding, in a dimension where love rules and the mind serves true love.

Love will always, always, find a way.

If she is ridiculed, it is an understandable, acceptable price. True love will never sing the songs of a hollow religion and is not pacified with pointless ritual. Love cannot coexist with legalism and does not interact well with hypocrisy.

If she is banished, it is a good thing, for it will allow more time to be with the Lord. If she is condemned, she will smile quietly, respectably, of course.

Condemnation is the last course of a clueless man.

Love cannot be condemned.

Love always prevails.

Love always gathers.

Love always forgives.

Love always heals.

Love understands.

Love feeds the world with compassion and mercy.

True love yields to the forgiving nature of her Lord and accurately represents His grace in every respect.

Love lives forever.

As for the stale complexities of religion, they will change. Someone possessing more courage than fear will face off with the ghosts of yesterday and the dusty echoes they represent, returning God's people to the simplicity and joy of loving God.

So, this is my journey, my quest. These are the notes of that quest. These are my encounters with the Divine along the way. I know some of the accounts that you are about to read will seem unreal. But let me encourage you to step out of the restraints of religious control. Let your spirit go. Give in to the yearning within, and come, let us romance the Divine together.

Who knows? We may find true love.

Section One

Chapter One

I remember the spectacular purity and unutterable beauty of His words to me. How gentle He was! How very gentle.

I saw things that I never dreamed or imagined, like that smile of His as He looked at me. It was so wonderful, so approving, almost as though He did not really know what was hidden inside of me. But that was the wonder of it all. He did know what was inside of me and still IS inside of me, and yet, He loved me in spite of it all.

I think that was the first time I stopped squirming as He held me in His arms. Wow. How many years did it take me to realize that it was a good thing to be in the Presence of God, to be held and loved by His Presence?

I must admit, though, at first I looked at Him a little warily. But it was only for a moment. We are taught to fear God in order to serve Him, that punishment is our lot as a Christian, and that no one will ever, ever see God's face and live. But there I sat, peering into this smiling face that obviously had not a trace of condemnation on it. And I lived. What was He up to? Why was He smiling at me, loving me, holding me, yet knowing fully what was lodged inside of me? His eyes were so clear. I could not stop staring at Him. I held my breath as I dared look deep into His heart. What a wonder! All I saw was love. Love and forgiveness for me, yes, but also for humanity. All humanity throughout all time. Who could ever imagine such a thing? How totally pure. How totally full of compassion and hope He was.

I looked for all that stuff the religious hucksters said was in God, but I couldn't see any of it there. There was no condemnation, no anger, and no memory of sin long ago repented for. There was only a longing for friendship, a desire for union with the likes of me. It began to shatter all my fears and preconceptions of who God was supposed to be.

But there was something else there I had never heard about…something no one had ever told me was in the heart of the Lord.

Amazing.

His heart was full of dreams. Dreams for me, dreams for each person who had ever been conceived. They were wonderful dreams, astonishing possibilities. Such mighty dreams they were, too! Dreams to win, to succeed, to flourish. Dreams to invent, to discover, to write! Dreams to change the thoughts of man, to lead nations, to raise children who would carry the torch of His Life to generations yet unborn. All these dreams were intricately and lovingly woven together into a tapestry of His will that transcended the ages and brought God's ultimate purpose for this planet into being. Surely only angels saw such wonders, or so I thought.

"You have such stunning dreams for us. Your plans are so awesome," I ventured to say to Him. "Why is it that, well, that…"

Chapter One

"That it doesn't seem to come to pass?" He finished the question I wanted to ask Him, but just couldn't. "The beauty of these dreams goes far beyond their outcome. Its beauty is birthed in the hearts of those who freely give themselves to say 'yes' to what I have for them. Of course, the dreams are sovereign, but I have no puppets, no slaves, no forced laborers. They are so pure that any intervention by fear or control would taint their beauty and destroy their intention. So I have been patiently waiting for you to respond, for you to say 'yes', to see purpose and fulfillment and beauty beyond yourself, beyond your own needs and wants."

Well, when I heard that, I found myself praying prayers I never thought I would ever hear myself pray.

"Lord, have Your way in me. I give myself to You. Please take control of my life. I want Your dreams for me to come to pass, every one of them. Thy kingdom come, Thy will be done—in me! Teach me to say 'yes'."

It was the first time I really believed that He loved me. It seemed that His love poured out of eternity itself with an orchestra of light and sound and hope and every possibility that a man can ever desire to contain.

There I sat in His arms, looking intently into His eyes—eyes so clear, so pure, that I could see to the depths of His heart.

"Come, My son, let Me show you My love for you. Let Me show you the power of eternity and what awaits you in this life. Let Me show you what 'yes' can do."

Immediately, I saw back into the beginning of something…or was it the middle of something? I guess I really do not know what place in time or out of time it was; all I knew was that I heard the very compassion of our Lord as He spoke words that seemed to transcend the ages:

"Who has believed our report? And to whom has the arm of the Lord been revealed?"

His words were so penetrating, so heart-piercing. I could see through the ages as His words seemed to fill the air with their power. They went out of His mouth like mighty arrows flying through eternity, breaking swiftly into time and space, as if on individual missions sent from the heart of the Lord Himself. His words swept through continents and blew over nations and peoples.

"For He grew up before Him as a tender plant, and as a root out of dry ground."

The gentleness and yet the urgency of His love was nearly more than I could contain as He proclaimed to His creation:

"He has no stately form or majesty that we should look at Him, and no beauty that we should be attracted to Him."

The inner melody of His tender love began to draw many people from every land and from every age. His words echoed with great determination and assurance as people responded to them. I watched His words being delivered to hearts without regard to times, epochs, nationalities, or governments and in spite of religions and institutions. Barriers between men began to crumble as I watched in total awe the wonder of the new birth taking place in the hearts of literally hundreds of millions of people throughout time. His words rattled the very foundations of the earth as He declared,

"He was despised and rejected by men, a man of sorrows and acquainted with grief. And like one from whom men hide their faces, He was despised, and we gave Him no esteem."

I could see more clearly now as my heart yielded to His. His words were not falling randomly; instead, each one was carefully captured and carried to an individual human soul—purposefully, lovingly, longingly. It was as though the Lord had addressed each word to a particular person in a methodical, carefully planned dissemination of His love for all the ages. Folks continued to come to Him. Beyond numbers they were responding to His mighty love.

He watched patiently as His Word transformed nation after nation in millennium after millennium. He paused with a great sigh as He looked out over the masses, over the nations throughout which the angels were being sent. A heaviness seemed to overwhelm Him as He cried out once again,

"Surely He has borne our griefs and carried our sorrow."

I never before understood how intensely love can empower or bring pain. Was it the pain of sorrow or was it the depths of His eternal love that caused Him to cry out with such determined finality?

"But He was wounded for our transgressions, He was bruised for our iniquities…"

Whatever moved Him, one thing was certain: The power of His love was unmistakably the greatest force in the universe. Neither time nor space could contain it. Law, theology, government, the pride or greed of man—none of it could withstand the convincing, penetrating splendor of His extraordinary love. Oh, the drawing power of His love as countless numbers were melted by His tenderness! So many were healed in all millennia! So many called upon Him in every time under the sun. One word spoken from the very Life of the Father did what no mere mortal man could ever hope to do, even in a lifetime. It was inconceivable to the human mind.

I was beginning to realize that I was privileged to see God's mighty power ignoring the boundaries of men and nations and time itself. Not even the constraints of nature could contain the determined love of an all-powerful God, a God who would pay the ultimate price for the redemption of a fallen, rebellious race. It was almost as though He had already felt the pain of releasing His Son to death so very long before it actually happened in time.

Yet His voice was commanding, His determination unflinching, His resolve unchangeable. His Word would reach everyone in every epoch. Everyone would hear, everyone would know, everyone could say "yes." His voice smashed the sacred theologies of carnal men as easily as He had broken through time.

"The chastisement for our peace was upon Him, and by His stripes we are healed."

Human words, in any language, cannot begin to describe the events that followed as more and more people fell to their knees, responding to this eternal love. Marriages were being mended, families were being restored, broken dreams were being recovered, entire nations were being drawn to His Light, and hope was being recaptured in the hearts of a myriad of new believers. Humanity was discovering the never-ending, never-failing compassion of our Lord who never stops wooing, never stops loving, and never, ever gives up on even the most stubborn of His children.

Then, almost on cue, the redeemed paused and looked up. With one powerful voice of gratefulness and thanksgiving, they began to worship the Lord with thunderous praise and a crescendo of worship that seemed to rock even the foundation of His mighty throne. The sound filled Heaven and resounded again and again back to the earth as the angels continued their systematic administration of His love throughout the earth without distraction, even in the midst of such a universal, multi-dimensional, time-ignoring shout of worship to Him who sits on the throne.

I found myself weeping for joy there in His Presence, watching the power of His Word perform all it was intended to do.

The Lord turned to me and spoke. "This is but the Door through which My people will experience eternity while they yet dwell in their mortal bodies. I have gathered a spiritual people for a destiny that you cannot yet comprehend."

Chapter Two

*L*ittle did I know that I was about to discover how small my own understanding of His love had become, or how He would show His compassion and mercy to the likes of someone like me.

"Keep watching, for this is not all I have for you." Then the Lord turned His hand toward me. Startled and shaken with fear, I was frozen with anticipation as He again carefully took me into His arms. He began to whisper into my ear such words of love that I did not expect.

"I was wounded also for you, My troubled child."

I did not want to look into His eyes. He had seen what I had so carefully hidden over many years. In fact, it was hidden for so many years that I had almost forgotten about it myself. The Lord looked at me with a twinkle in His eye. "Tell them the truth," He said gently. He held me close. He knew how much it was about to hurt. "Tell your readers how it really has been. You never 'almost forgot.' In fact, you have been tormented day and night for more years than you can remember."

Then without warning, and certainly out of my control, old feelings welled up into my heart. Pain that I had not felt in a long, long time came crashing back into my mind. Memories long forgotten—okay, not forgotten, but certainly suppressed—began their relentless replays, just as before. Just as they always had done. I was suddenly imprisoned again. After so long a time of relief, I was trapped again. That is, until the Lord spoke to me through the power of His own resolve to see me whole. With indescribable gentleness, the Lord reached out His hands to me.

"Trapped again? Are you trapped again?" Not knowing how to respond, I remained quiet.

"You are not trapped again; you were never free from these things. You had only suppressed them and run from them, hoping that they would disappear. But My love for you is much greater than that. You would have spent the rest of your life wondering why I apparently did not care about the pain you were going through. You would have spent the rest of your life doubting My complete, uncompromising care for you. And I could not have that, now could I?

"Everything you would have thought and done would have been tainted with that nagging doubt. It would have haunted you and obscured your judgment. That is why you hesitate with uncertainty when you want to encourage someone. It is why you hold back when you want to move on in your experience with Me. I know you wonder if all My promises are really true. You even hesitate at My direction for your life. No, this is not My plan for you. This is no way to go through life. No, no, I want you to be free. I want you to understand that evil men who do not submit to My Lordship misuse the free will I give them. I gave mankind a free will not to do as they please, but to explore the depths of My love. I want you to joyously and freely explore the many gifts and opportunities I have placed within you, using them to bring happiness to others and fulfillment to yourself. I never intended for man to use his divinely given freedom to abuse others who also want to search the magnitude of My love for themselves."

Suddenly, all the years of doubt and frustration welled up from within. I looked at Him quizzically. Could this be true? With a smile that lit up the very depth of my heart, He held me to Himself. I could not ignore it. I could not hold in the pain any longer. Finally I could release it without fear. He knew how I felt! He knew what I was afraid to admit! He knew I was so afraid that just maybe He didn't really love me.

I thought I was dirty. I thought all these things had disqualified me from His love and from His plan for me. But now I know. Now I do not have to be afraid that He will let me down. He never turned His back on me. He never planned this for my life. From the moment those horrible things began to happen, He set out a plan for my deliverance. I will ever be thankful for what He has done.

"Oh, My afflicted and storm-tossed loved one."

His words penetrated my innermost being. He held me close and spoke softly into my ear, and I knew He wanted to heal me and take away all the pain.

"I will put your life in order like precious jewels. I will lay your foundations in sapphires. I will protect you with walls made out of rubies and gates made out of crystal.

"I am telling you the truth; everything about you will be made of gems. When someone looks at you, all that they will see will be precious. Your entire being will be a sight to behold, glistening in the Son."

I began to weep uncontrollably in His arms. Only He could know how I have longed to hear those words whispered into the depths of my heart. Only He could utter such words, allowing my own spirit to soar with His.

But I still could not control the flow of my tears. They flowed out like a great river. His words echoed again and again in my mind. I did not have to be strong and all alone anymore. There was One who was strong for me. There was One who cared for me and who was here for me now. I was like a sponge soaking up His love and His healing balm. My mind raced back to all the years of fear and condemnation, to the times I...I...did not want to remember. But I could face them now. I could face even the most painful times. As those memories flooded my heart, new pain, and even more sobbing, welled up from within. But something was happening. The more I remembered, the more He loved me. His Presence gathered me to Himself, literally taking away the pain of the past.

"O Lord, how I have longed for this day. How I have longed to know that You loved me and wanted to heal me. I have worked myself to exhaustion trying to prove myself to You, trying to convince You that I am worth healing, worth saving, worth loving." My tears poured like a waterfall. "But all the proving never seemed to be enough. It was as though I could do nothing to convince You." I could not help a sense of bitterness as I said these words to my Lord. For I had worked. I had done everything everyone had ever told me I had to do to have His favor. But nothing seemed to work. "I am so sorry, Lord, but You are such a taskmaster. You demand so much, I can never have Your favor."

It did not take long for the Lord to respond. "Religious taskmasters know little of My love and nothing of My favor. But you are right. You can never win My favor." Well, I was in shock. "Then how is it that I feel Your love and favor..." He stopped me before I said something I would regret.

"You do not understand, My son. Before the beginning of time, I saw you. I loved you. I dreamed about you. When I wove you in your mother's womb, gave you the color of your hair and your eyes; when I gave you your smile and your sense of humor and wove integrity into the very fiber of your being; when I secretly placed destiny within you and decided on your personality, your gender, your skin color; when I gave you gifts and talents and displayed you to the universe, you had My favor, My love, My desire.

"You can never work for what is already yours, for what I have already dreamed for you. From now on, your work is over. Your warfare is over. Rest in the arms of My love. Let me unfold My dream for you."

Like a great spiritual wash, His Presence began to clear away the pain and the struggle of yesterday.

"He healed me because He loved me. He loved me, well, because He did."

The healing balm of His Presence washed over me again and again and again. The memories were still there, but the pain was gone. It was being taken away by Him who alone has the power to heal and to restore to wholeness. And He did it because He loved me. For no other reason. I did not have to work for it, claim it, memorize it, or fast for it. He did not need me to convince Him of anything. It was His good pleasure to heal me.

After what seemed to be several hours, though I do not know really how long it was, I wiped my eyes and with blurry amazement realized that the Lord still held me in His arms, looking so lovingly right through to my spirit.

I realized also that we were walking. Well, He was walking and carrying me. We were both quiet for the longest time. I drifted off to a deep sleep in the warmth of His arms and the gentle rocking of His walk.

Suddenly we came to a stop. I awoke at the warning of His voice. "Get ready!" Then He laughed gently, "This may be cold." Without another word, we slipped into a cool, swiftly moving river. The water was so delicious, so clear. I easily saw to the bottom. As the crystal waters engulfed me, His face broke into a smile that would brighten a thousand midnights. "Are you ready?" He asked, as though something was about to happen.

Before I could say anything, and while He was still holding me tightly, we plunged underwater and He twirled me around and around. Bubbles surged and broke all around us. The swirling was making the water form little rivulets over His face as He watched me with an eye of grand anticipation. The water was washing away every vestige of my tears—and with them went all the uncertainty and doubt of His love for me. Ahhh, I never thought I could ever feel this way again as I rested totally in His arms without ever a fear that He would let me go. It was incredible, unbelievable. "So this is what it means to be free?" I tried to shout to Him over the sound of the water. But He did not respond. He only closed His eyes and continued to swirl me in the waters. *My, my. His yoke is easy. His burden is light*, I thought to myself.

Chapter Two

You know, if it hadn't been for the breathing thing, I could have stayed under that river all day with my Lord. But it ended way too soon. As quickly as we had plunged into the depths of the river, we came to the surface once again.

I could not tell if it was the water from the river or tears coming down His face. The ecstasy of the moment had brought a fresh deluge down my own face. But it was not fear or sorrow or pain this time; it was joy, the joy of the Lord deep, deep in my heart. I did not understand how or why, but I knew that He was *for* me. I knew I could believe Him. I knew that from now on, the battle was not mine, the pain was not mine, the torment was not mine. I was free to be all that God had dreamed for me to be. And more than that, I was free to love Him the way my soul yearned to love Him.

Now destiny took on a whole new meaning. I knew where I wanted to be, where I wanted to live, and whom I wanted to follow. Destiny no longer had anything to do with what I did, but where I lived and whom I loved. I would do anything for Him. I would go anywhere for Him just as long as I did not have to move from this place of the Presence. Destiny would never again be a matter of career or professional training. My destiny would be to live in the "yes" of God.

Gently He brought me to the side of the river where He laid me against a huge tree that seemed to wrap itself around me, reassuring me of His love. Its roots dove hungrily deep into the ground as though it knew the richness and power of the river that swirled beside it.

I wonder how many others this tree has comforted over the years? I thought silently. I was startled when the Lord answered my unspoken question with a broad smile, "More than you can count."

I smiled back at Him. This was such an awesome place. So safe, so secure, so private. And of course, He was there.

Angels came from everywhere tending to the needs of the Lord, and much to my surprise, to my needs as well. They gently pulled leaves from the tree and laid them upon my brow, bringing an assuring warmth and calmness to my mind and a peace to the deepest recesses of my heart. I knew that things would never be the same again. Even though years of fear and frustration screamed to me, insisting that all would return as it had been before much time had passed, I knew it would be different. The pain no longer dictated how I felt or what I believed. It was gone. Its power had been broken. Now, I knew who was Lord. I knew whose voice I would listen to.

As I lay against this magnificent tree, night began to fall. The Lord began to speak to several of the angels who were nearby. They listened to Him carefully, occasionally nodding as He spoke and gestured with His hands. One of the angels slowly turned his eyes toward me, momentarily catching my glance, but quickly turned back to the Lord. Soon, their instructions apparently complete, they flew off in every direction.

The Lord stood alone for a moment in the twilight, then turned and walked in my direction. The dew was falling now, and the dampness sent a chill through my entire body.

The Lord noticed my tremble and quickly summoned an angel to build a fire. The Lord turned to me and smiled as the warmth of the fire reached my face. I smiled back without a word.

I was glad for the fire. In every direction there was only darkness...darkness and silence...except, of course, for the sound of the rushing waters that had healed me that day. But even that was only a sound, for the darkness had engulfed everything. I had never been here before; the land was new to me, but I understood darkness. Oh yes, I knew darkness and the fear it would normally bring to my heart. I had no idea what to expect next, but I trusted Him, that was certain. Yes, for the first time in my life, that was certain.

He knelt down in front of me and took my face ever so gently into His hands. "I have longed for you to hear Me say this to you, My son." He carefully leaned over me and whispered into my ear, "I will never leave you; I will never give up on you. My love for you is too great. I will not permit the enemy to win." More quickly than I could ever understand, His precious words flowed inside and gripped the deepest recesses of my heart. It was a moment I would always cherish. It was one I would relive again and again as He took me deeper into His heart.

Then, with a rush of wind, hundreds of angels surrounded me. These did not fly as the others. These rode the most wonderful horses anyone could imagine. The thundering of hooves startled me for a moment, but since the Lord was with me, what could I fear? These horses were wonderful animals. They were alert and poised, pawing the ground with ears swiveled back. They snorted and moved their heads impatiently, anxiously awaiting a command from their riders.

These angels were different from all the other ones I had seen. These were solemn and intense in their manner, carrying swords and shields and taking up positions on both sides of me. Some of the horses were skittish as a few angels rode off to the rear with their swords drawn and their shields up.

"Hold your places!" the Lord's voice abruptly broke the silence. With one animated motion, He was on His horse. With only a gesture of His eyes, He sent several angels off quickly into the darkness. The Lord was about to follow the angels who had just disappeared.

I became frightened when I saw the fire in my Lord's eyes and I cried out, "Lord, where are You going? What is happening?" The Lord pulled back on His reins and the horse came to a stop. As quickly as He had mounted, He was off the horse. In a moment of time He was kneeling again in front of me. His eyes blazed with compassion and anger. His hair had blown partially in His face. His clothes wrapped Him like a pillar of fire. He pointed His finger at me with great assurance and comfort. His voice shook with determination. The angels winced at His resolve. They looked at one another as though to say, "We have heard this before!"

I was sure I was about to die as I heard His thunderous voice directed toward me. "No weapon formed against you will flourish. If anyone fiercely attacks you, I will attack him. And every tongue that tries to accuse you of the things that I have forgiven you for, you will stand up and condemn them!" With those mighty words, He turned away. But before I could even allow those words to sink into my heart, He turned around once more, the fire still raging in His eyes. "This is your heritage because I love you. I have promised to take care of you!"

He then turned and mounted His horse. He looked to me once again as He rode off, shouting with great victory, "Your vindication will always be from Me. You have nothing to fear." With those words, He rode off at a full gallop. I watched until He disappeared into the darkness.

Chapter Two

Dozens of angels seemed to follow Him into the darkness. *Should I get up? Is there something to be afraid of?* I wondered to myself. I jumped to my feet as if there would have been something I could do to defend myself. I looked around the clearing, certain that something was about to come lunging out of the darkness.

My imagination was in full gear when an angel, standing by the fire, noticed that I had stood. In less than a moment, he was at my side with a reassuring look of confidence.

"There is nothing to be afraid of," he began.

"But the Lord rode off in such a hurry. It was as though He was going into battle."

"Precisely why you have nothing to worry about."

A wonderful calm poured over me as the angel spoke.

"Of course, that is exactly why I have nothing to fear."

The angel walked me back to the tree. I sat with new confidence. An angel stood on either side of the tree, guarding me. I looked up to one of them, who spoke before I could.

"We will be here with you throughout the night."

It was quiet again, but I was far from alone. Not only was I guarded on either side by angels, but everywhere I looked, angels kept watch over me. I knew I was safe. I knew that whatever was out there that made the Lord ride off so quickly, would not be able to come near me. With that thought lingering in my mind, I fell into a deep sleep.

Chapter Three

The morning chill made me shiver as I awoke on the riverbank. A pale mist rose from the water as the sun shot its first rays through the trees of this unknown woodland. I could see birds flying from tree to tree, but their songs were drowned by the rushing of the river. Angels still guarded the clearing. A fire still burned close by. The crackling of the fire and the warmth of its flames offered a pleasant and reassuring reminder of the night before and the peace the Lord had brought to my heart. An angel served me hot tea and warm bread, thus completing this idyllic morning.

I had not seen Him since He rode off several hours earlier, but somehow, I knew He was near.

The memory of the night before was so sweet. Some folks may have wondered if it was all just a dream, or maybe just the work of an overactive imagination. I knew better. This was not my imagination.

I had been a believer for many years. I thought I knew the power of His love. But last night was remarkable. I could never deny it; nor could anyone explain it away. I knew what I had experienced; I knew what I saw, what I heard, what I touched. No one could take that away from me. I had passed from death into life, from despair into hope, from guilt into freedom. *He did say that His burden was easy and His load light,* I thought to myself. *But this is wonderful, far more than I could ever have expected.* I am afraid I gloated in my newfound sense of acceptance and love from the Lord. "Now this, this is 'born again'!"

As the heat of the fire radiated to my face, the chill passed away. I smiled as I thought about the night before.

Forgiveness was certainly the highlight of the evening. I had truly experienced mercy along with the unbelievable freedom from guilt that comes with true forgiveness. Yes, the guilt was gone, really gone. I mean, *gone,* exactly the way it was gone when I first gave my heart to Him so many years ago. No wonder it felt like I had passed from death to life. In a very real way, I had. Guilt is the cloud, the reminder, the fear of death, in spite of what religious doctrines may tell you otherwise.

Yes, I had repented countless times for my sins. I had begged the Lord to remove the shame, the hounding guilt of it all.

But this was different. This was like nothing else I had done. This time I responded to Him and Him alone. I did not need someone telling me how to repent or how to feel after I had repented. I did not look for the approval of men, nor would I respond to the demands for "evangelical purgatory" just to be sure I had worked off any intention to sin again. No one would be my judge. The pain of sinning before the One whom my soul loves would keep me broken, humble, repentant. His Presence would encourage me, strengthen me, and assure me of His love and forgiveness. My relationship was with Him, not with a system of religious mortification intended to keep me fearful, lonely, and guilty.

Chapter Three

My life had been forever changed. I had no intention of going back to the way it was. I knew some would call me rebellious, out of control, and divisive. But I had found Him. What could man really do to me?

When I had first cried out to Him many years ago, it had been with that same desperation. I remember those days as though they were yesterday. They were wonderful days, marvelous in every way. I had discovered that God loved me. I did not care who heard, who understood, or what people would say. It did not matter what friends I would lose or how folks might ridicule me for the way I simply talked to God and the way my life changed because of it. I wanted Him, I wanted to be free, and I wanted my life to make a difference. I was tired of seeing time pass and my purpose for being here pass with it. There was more to life, more to God than merely the weekly trips to church. When I first talked to the Lord, I talked as though my whole future, my whole existence depended on it, because it did. I did not use a formula prayer. Nor did I pray someone else's prayer. I just talked to Him—desperately, earnestly, honestly, repentantly. I did not know if it met with anyone's approval, but I did not really care. I had to talk to God. I had to know His love, His forgiveness, His mercy. I had to know I mattered to Him. I had to tell Him that He mattered to me and that I wanted to serve Him. I wanted my life to mean something.

The world could go to hell.

I would do what I knew was right. I would call upon God openly, freely, and without restraint.

So, the more I thought about it, maybe this time was not so much different after all. For again, I was desperate for Him. Once again, I did not care what others would say. It did not matter what I was taught, what I was told to believe, or what someone else thought I should believe. I had heard enough Bible-thumping sermons, and I had preached enough Bible-thumping sermons.

I was, and still am, a hungry man.

I need Him. I want Him.

I will call upon Him.

I will go into His Presence. If it costs me my life, so be it.

I am dying anyway.

I was a little shocked at my own resolve, wondering where these thoughts had been. Were they new? Had they been hidden? Were they to guide me and control me from now on? I hoped so. They were good thoughts, exhilarating thoughts, to be sure. It is amazing what surfaces once fear and guilt are done away with. Now there is nothing to hold me back, nothing to keep me from the One I love so desperately.

But I really am desperate. I am desperate for what is real, for what is relevant. I am weary of structures and the hyperbole of all the very important things we have tried to do, hoping to interest a bored and frustrated Church while the world passed by bankrupt in soul and spirit. No, I need Jesus in all His radical love and His disreputable sense of mercy to the likes of struggling folks like me.

I have had enough of the religious elite bemoaning the power of the nation's political leaders as though they are any different. I have had enough threats of damnation by these elite few. You know the ones. They condemn you if you do not believe as they have established you should believe. But they themselves recklessly interpret God's Word in a villainous attempt to secure their own legalistic empires. They do not care that the rest of us struggle hopelessly to reach their damnable standard of righteousness that God Himself does not require.

No, this is not the Church. At least, this is not the Church that Jesus is building. His Church is far different from the system we have become used to calling the Church. This religious system is really only an aberration of the reality of His Life living and moving and existing in all His wonderfulness in human beings.

This anomaly of the true Church has a foundation of rules, regulations, and laws that they strap upon the backs of sincere and seeking believers, keeping them tired, confused, and far from their Lord. They pronounce edicts, "Do not handle, do not taste, do not touch!" It all sounds so good, and it even made me feel good, but it did nothing to stop fleshly cravings and temptations. These lifeless rules are heavy indeed, and they breed disillusionment and hopelessness among God's people.

Self-abasement may work for a season, but I had grown weary battling the relentless temptations that never seemed to need rest and never gave me a break. It is a continuous and daily fight that mere mortal man is destined to lose.

These controls of a religious system are a sure sign that the Presence of God is not among them and probably is not welcome. The only truly permanent help against the struggles of our humanity is the vibrant, interactive, loving Presence of the Lord. He alone strengthens us in the struggle and brings final deliverance. When He is not among us as a normal experience, the only resort is legalism and threats of condemnation.

This system will take control wherever it can. When it detects sincerity and genuine purity of heart, it begins crafting deceptive authenticity to its own interpretation of the purity growing in the heart of the believer. Crafting ungodly loyalty to a system of religion that will never bring the earnest seeker into the Kingdom of God, the religious system preys on the humble sincerity of those who genuinely call upon the Lord. Religion demands attendance to comatose services, forgetting that the Presence of God is the magnet that would draw the masses. Religion's fleshly attempts to cast guilt upon those who sense lifelessness but are bound by guilt and fear would not be necessary if He were in the midst of them. Religion creates spiritually empty mimes who go through the motions of true holiness and spirituality but have no substance within. It creates leaders who spend their energy writing and enforcing laws of dress, attendance, loyalty, conduct, or association. These fearful and insecure leaders tell you who you may befriend and who you may not. Under the disguise of protecting the flock from the evils of society and the "carnal" church, their doctrines separate us from the very people Jesus came to redeem.

Such leaders would do well to sincerely ask the Lord for the freedom in Christ their flocks also yearn for. Although it is certain that many are a product of their own denominational doctrines and lifeless rhetoric, it does not free them of their responsibility to seek Him in Spirit and truth who, after all, is life and power in Himself.

They build walls between believers based on peripheral doctrines. They spend their time in discussion and condemnation of those who are different in custom and theology even though these different folks embrace the love of God in Christ Jesus. They totally miss the point that Jesus is a gathering, not a scattering Redeemer. Enforcing this false sense of loyalty was successful only because of the believers' profound sense of respect and dedication to the Lord and His shepherds.

But now, now something new is happening in me. I am growing in courage. I am listening to the voice of the Lord who resides within my heart and covets friendship with me as I do with Him.

Meanwhile, I was so caught in my thoughts that I did not notice an angel preparing food for me. I stood for a moment to stretch my legs a bit. As I sat down again, he placed a blanket beside me, along with a pot of steaming broth.

The angel just sat in front of me smiling. I guessed he was waiting for me to eat.

Maybe he has never seen a human eat before, I thought to myself. *On the other hand, maybe he is hungry and is waiting for me to invite him to join me.*

On the other hand, maybe angels do not eat. I felt a hand on my shoulder as the Lord looked at me, quite amused.

"Do not be uneasy with his presence; he is here to serve you, nothing more."

"Oh, oh, thank You, Lord." I turned back to the angel, a little embarrassed at my clumsy response to his service to me.

"Than you, too. I am quite hungry, you know. It smells wonderful."

"You are quite welcome. You had better eat it while it is still hot and tasty," the angel responded.

"Yes, yes, of course. I will."

I do not understand what was so fascinating about someone drinking broth, but my guard remained, watching intently, until I had finished the nourishing liquid.

I was enjoying my time there in the clearing. The musings of my heart were revealing and intense. They challenged my core beliefs and urged me to venture out of the confines of mere religion and into the open spaces of love and relationship with my Lord.

I heard the Lord speak to me again.

"Take My yoke upon you and learn of Me, for My yoke is easy and My burden is light."

It was amazing to hear the Lord speak. Everyone can quote the words of the Lord, but not many of us actually believe them.

After all the wearisome things that we have been taught are so necessary, who will believe the liberating report of the Lord?

Who will believe it can be so easy?

I will.

I have come to only one conclusion. Since I have been raised with Christ, I will believe Him. I will continue to seek the things that are above, where He dwells, at the right hand of God. I am going to seek the things that flow from His throne and His throne alone. Yes, I will fail along the way. I will sin again. But I also will repent again. And He will forgive me again. I will draw close to Him in spite of myself, and He will deliver me from all my unrighteousness. He is working inside of me while I am serving Him. I am free from condemnation and the accusations of those who sit in the seat of the scornful. I will follow the Lord.

And yes, I do not care what they say or how they accuse or how they dis-fellowship. And yes, I know it will cost me friends as it did in the beginning. It will cost me my reputation as it did in the beginning. But I will gain Him who lives outside the controls of religion and the rules that these modern Pharisees establish in their feeble, fleshly attempts to legitimize their own kingdom-building efforts.

They call the hungry and the thirsty heretics—an accusation that flows far too easily from the lips of the sages of a lifeless and morbid system of religious ideology that has no power, no truth, and certainly no savior.

It just doesn't matter anymore. The voice of mere mortal man sounds so different than the voice of my Beloved. Every time I hear "God didn't," it most likely means He did. When I hear someone say, "God doesn't," I am sure that He does. "God won't" or "God can't" without question means He will and He does.

I have found Him again, and I will not allow Him to slip away to become lost once more in a religious black hole of mediocrity and death.

So yes, this time is much like the first time I called upon Him. Just like before, I prayed like my whole future, my whole existence depended on it, because it did. I did not consult a doctrinal correctness manual before I prayed. Nor did I read a prayer that may have worked for someone else.

I just got real risky. I talked to Him in my own words, desperately, earnestly, honestly, repentantly. I did not know if it met with anyone's approval, but I did not really care. I had to talk to God. I had to know His love, His forgiveness, His mercy, again. I had to know I still mattered to Him. I had to tell Him that He still mattered to me and that I wanted to serve Him. I wanted my life to mean something. The church system could go to hell. I would do what I knew was right. I would call upon God openly, freely, and without restraint.

And then? Well, then I would wait. If I was wrong, it would be no big loss. Everyone was so certain my words were just the thoughts of a rebellious, insubordinate radical anyway. But if I was right—if I was right—then things would be different. Then the whole world would change, beginning with my own.

As I thought about these issues of my heart, I began to feel a new joy and power welling up from within. I laughed as I watched the angels in this small clearing. How real this realm of eternity is! How silly are our human efforts to deny its awesome power and existence. I could almost feel the restraints dropping from my mind and spirit. After so many years, I had finally touched the eternity of God, for I touched God. It really is funny, you know. So much time is spent trying to explain away the reality of this dimension that is infinitely more powerful than the one we live in. It is no wonder to me that no human words, no human doctrines or intellectual dissertations, no frightened and insecure men can talk away what has been from eternity past and will exist to eternity future. Humanity does not possess the vocabulary to snuff out the fire of His Life that burns with such consuming brilliance in the hearts of His people around the world.

How ironic. We will argue creationism to the secular world, but we deny the power of the dimension we so vehemently believe created the world and all it contains.

So anyway, here I sat, watching angels, so real, so tangible, so protective. I had peace that I had not experienced in years; I had freedom from guilt, freedom from heavy burdens...it was as though I could fly, I was so light. Who would not want this salvation, this forgiveness for this life as well as the next?

"Jesus, if this is what Your Kingdom brings, then absolutely I will pray with You, 'Thy kingdom come, Thy will be done, on earth as it is in heaven.' Absolutely, Lord. This is what I want. My loyalty is to You, the only One who can accomplish this in the earth; the only One who can build the Church; the only One whose burden is light and marvelous and enticing and beautiful and glorious and eternal. You have my heart. You really do."

The sun shone through the trees as I prayed. The wind gently blew over me, carrying the scent of what seemed to be honeysuckle. I nearly drifted off to sleep...

Chapter Four

"**W**here are your thoughts?" the Lord asked gently. His hand was on my shoulder. His eyes were compassionate, full of love and understanding as always. I tried to hide that I was startled as I gathered myself from my drifting feelings. I responded rather stupidly, "Oh, Lord...don't You know?"

He smiled back, "Of course I know. I just want to be certain that you know." He sat near to me so He could look directly into my eyes. There was a time when that would have frightened me. Now I love His nearness.

"I want to be sure you understand the danger of using your past to guide your future," He started gently. I guess I looked rather perplexed as He smiled right into my heart, so He continued.

"You can never center the course of your future on the ridicule and pain of your past. Yesterday will always send mixed signals of rejection, anger, envy, confusion, and revenge. Setting your future course from the view of what has happened to you will never give you a clear course to follow. You will spend your future trying to prove your tormentors wrong."

"But Lord, these tormentors have kept me from You for many years."

"This is what I want you to do." He seemed to ignore my little interruption. "I want you to forgive those whom you need to forgive. Release them from your judgment. Set them free. In fact, in some instances, you should thank them. They are the ones whom I sent to harass you to the point where you would be willing to move forward into the new things I have for you."

I dropped my head. It was so embarrassing. I like to think that the desire to follow the Lord was mine. But He had to give even this to me. He was right, of course. I only ran to Him because I ran from something. Now I know we all start there, but it is still rough on the ego.

The Lord continued His gentle instruction.

"Now give these people, relationships, and memories to Me. Give the pain of your past to Me. What is it to you if I decide to forgive them? I will deal with them as you would want Me to deal with you: with love, mercy, compassion, and healing. I will change them as I am changing you. Leave them in My hands. You must move on. Do not drag them with you in your anger and pain. They are baggage you definitely do not need."

Of course, He was right. As usual, I might add. I had come too far to begin to argue with Him now. Besides, it is much easier to say "yes" to Him, even if I do not understand.

"Now then, My dear son, look to Me. Let Me draw you into My life, My love, My mercy, and My strength. Keep your eyes on Me. I mean, directly on Me. I will draw you to Myself. The work of human flesh only confuses the process. Yield to Me. Rest in Me. Trust in Me. I know the times, the seasons, the hopes, the dreams. I will bring it to pass at the right time. Do not fret the passing of time. Whatever your hands find to do, do with all your heart as unto Me. I hold your future in My heart. I will not let it fall to the ground."

"But time moves so quickly, I do not want to miss anything You have for me."

"Men, even men with evil intentions, cannot rob you of the dreams I have for you. You have no need to force your own way, build your own signs, write your own résumé. I promote at the right time. Just rest in Me. You are in the palm of My hand." His words were so gentle, so penetrating, so lovely.

"I believe You, Lord. I believe You. I will do as You have said. And...and...thank You. Thank You, Lord."

He smiled again, hugged me with one of those hugs that says "I love you too" in a thousand ways, and turned to go.

"But, Lord, where are You going?"

He continued to walk as though He had not heard me.

"Lord, I am here on this riverbank in a wood I do not know. What is to become of me now? What should I do?"

The Lord returned to me and knelt down in front of me. He took my hands as He spoke.

"You must cross the river."

"*I* must cross the river?" I did not know why that thought sent such fear through my heart, but it did.

"*I* must cross the river...alone?"

The Lord smiled with hopeful confidence. "You must cross the river."

"*Alone?*" I replied in unbelief.

"There is far more for you on the other side of the river. But do not be afraid; I will be with you," the Lord said softly.

"Okay, let's go…You and me. I'm ready to go!" I am afraid I was not nearly as composed as He was. " I do not seem to see the problem here, Lord. You want to go, I want to go…let's go!"

The Lord looked confidently into my eyes, as though I had no clue what I had just decided to do. And I didn't. "I agree. Let's go." He reached for my hand and pulled me up from the ground and from the tree I was lying against.

I was startled by how cold it seemed once I was up. We walked silently toward the river. We were much farther from the bank than I had realized. It was so loud. It seemed as though I could have reached into the water from where I sat. But we were quite far from the river. And the closer we got, the louder it became. By the time we were actually at the bank, the sound of the rushing current was deafening. Then I realized why I was so nervous.

"This is not the place, is it? Is there an easier place to cross?" I had to shout for Him to hear me. "Let's cross where we entered the river last night," I suggested nervously.

"This *is* where we entered last evening."

"But it *can't* be. It was so calm, so gentle, last night."

"This is where we entered," the Lord reassured me. "You were just in a more trusting frame of mind last evening."

"But I do not remember all these rocks and rapids and noise. I…I did not notice them last night."

"That is because you were not looking at them last night. You were looking at Me."

"Well, I am still looking at You, Lord, I really am. But, is there an easier place to cross? A safer place?"

"No, there is no other place to cross." He said rather matter-of-factly. "This is where we cross."

"This is where we cross," I repeated to myself. "This is where we cross," I said a second time as I gazed into the whirling surge below. I just stared. I took a deep breath in a futile attempt to regain my composure. I repeated His words calmly once again. "This is where we cross." But I could not do it. I turned to Him, trembling. "This is where we cross?"

"This is where we cross." He squeezed my hand as He repeated Himself yet again.

The waters heaved and surged against the bank. They carried dirt and silt and the fragments of a thousand tree branches that had been splintered by the strength of this rushing torrent. I watched breathlessly as the water churned up mud and sand and smacked them effortlessly against the bank.

"Oh, I get it. We get to walk *on* the water! Wow, Lord, I always wanted to walk on water. This will be…"

"No," He said, looking into my eyes. "We do not get to walk on water. We must walk through it."

"We must walk through it? We must walk through this river to get to the other side?"

"Well, more correctly, *you* must walk through the river to get to the other side."

"I must walk through the water myself? You are not coming? I have to do this? I thought You would go with me. I thought we would go across the river together, You know, just You and me, just the two of us?"

"I am already on the other side."

"You are standing here with me, how can You be on the other...side?" My question drifted away quietly.

It suddenly worked its way through my mind. My eyes turned slowly away from Him and into the angry waters below.

"He is already on the other side..."

The river suddenly seemed to roar louder than ever as its current crashed against the bank and splintered logs as though they were nothing. The white foam from the waves was dirty as it ground sediment from the bottom and thrust it to the surface, only to be pulled down once again by the heaving waters.

I thought to myself, *This is the veil. This is my humanity, my fleshly self. This is the Cross. This is what He passed through for my sake. The pain, the suffering, the rejection, the torment that He suffered is all here before me.*

The Lord interrupted my thoughts. "Shall I take you to the edge?"

Before I could say, "no," we were at the water's edge. The Lord stepped in ahead of me. The waters swirled around Him as He turned to face me. I followed Him in until I seemed to lose my balance. The Lord quickly reached His hand to mine as I shouted in fear.

"Take My hand," the Lord called to me over the sound of the rushing waters. But I had already backed away to a rather safe distance on the shore. He smiled a rather confident smile when He saw that I had backed away. He reached out His hands to me and beckoned me to come. "I will never leave you. Come with Me. Put your faith in Me. I will satisfy you far more than the human comforts you fear to leave behind."

"Uhh…well…I need to think about this some." I needed a way to stall Him for a few minutes to get my thoughts together. "Uhh, Lord, I need to pray about this."

That was not the right thing to say.

"You need to pray about this?" The Lord repeated my question. "You need to pray about this? To whom? Look, every joy, every fulfillment is on the other side of your humanity. I am there to love you, to free you of your enemies once and for all. I came to put your war to an end, to free you to serve Me as your heart desires, to satisfy your deepest hope of serving Me."

In less than a moment, He was on the other side calling to me, singing to me, holding His arms out to me. I could feel the power of His love like never before. It was like a magnet, drawing me, wooing me to Himself. *He wants me to come over.* I inched a little closer to the water. My knees were getting weak, and my heart was pounding hard.

"He wants me cross the river," I mumbled over and over to myself.

"Now where is all your courageous resolve?" I scolded myself. "All that stuff sounds good until you get to a place like this."

"Lord, excuse me. Isn't this where all the giants live?" I called to Him. "I remember that the giants are in the Promised Land. I think they want to kill me. Don't they live there?"

In less than a moment He was standing in front of me. "Come over here, sit with Me, and I will make these giants, these monsters that torment you, a footstool for you. These things that you are so sure cannot be defeated are coming down. I promise. I will be with you."

But out of the corner of my eye I could see these enemies of mine gathering on the other side, just where Jesus had been standing a moment ago. They laughed and pointed their accusing fingers in my direction.

"He has no strength to follow his Lord," they mocked. "Sure, he looks strong now, but what will he do when is left all alone with no one to help him? What will he do then?" they continued to chide.

A shiver ran up my back.

Then I heard the Lord. "But that is the point, My son. I am not going to leave you. I will always be here."

"No fair, no fair!" A whining voice called from across the water. "We do not know what He is saying to you. How do you know He is telling you the truth if we cannot confirm His words to you?"

"He is probably lying," another voice chimed in. "You can never trust the Lord. He never answers your prayers the way you want Him to! What makes Him the expert on what is best for your life?"

I took a deep breath and wrapped my arms around the Lord.

"Oh, now look at the sissy. A grown person hanging on God. Isn't that sweet," one enemy taunted. "What's the matter? Can't you stand up for yourself? What's the matter with feeling good about yourself, anyway?"

I buried my face into the Lord's chest. The beating of His heart calmed me. Then I felt the Lord taking a deep breath. He lifted His face from my head and glanced briefly across the river. In less than an instant, my enemies were gone.

"Thank You, Lord. I am so sorry for those tormentors. Please forgive me."

"No, no," the Lord said encouragingly. "You did very well."

"I did?" I responded with a little shock.

"Of course you did, My son. Too many people run in shame from Me when their enemies show their ugly faces. They think I will be angry."

"But those guys said some awful things about You, Lord."

"I can handle it." The Lord smiled back at me. "The most important thing is that you did not run from Me. Had you run, your tormentors would have had you for days, chasing you all over the riverside. But you buried your fear in Me. You trusted Me, so I could chase them away." Then the Lord changed His tone. He became resolute in His stance, squinting His eyes and extending His jaw.

"But, My son, once you cross the river, I will destroy them one by one, once and for all. They will never bother you again." He turned to look into my anxious eyes. "That is My commitment to your well-being."

"Now," the Lord smiled at me, "where were we?"

"I didn't want to cross the river, and then I saw my enemies and You came across the river..."

"Yes, yes, I remember.

"Last night you discovered the power of My forgiveness," He said. "This morning you gave Me your heart. Now I want to give you the strength and courage to give Me your will, your future, your destiny. Now I will show you the power of My deliverance."

In spite of what I had just experienced, a sense of fear still gripped me.

"No, no. I think they are still over there hiding in the brush. I am so sorry, but I believe they will always be there. I just do not think there is hope for me."

"Neither did Israel when I delivered her from bondage."

"But that was different," I protested.

"Oh, it was?" the Lord asked.

Suddenly, the plight of the children of Israel did not seem so foolish. Suddenly I understood how they could be delivered from Egypt but frozen by fear when it came time to enter the Promised Land, when it came time to trust that the Lord would free them from the giants that occupied their inheritance.

Indeed, we were very much the same.

Chapter Five

The Lord took my arm and walked me back to the tree without a word. He sat next to me there with His arm firmly around my shoulder. It seemed as though His thoughts were miles or dimensions away.

I was afraid to speak to Him. The angels were there, as usual, to minister to our needs. I watched absently as they went about their chores. I wondered if they knew how I had just failed. I wondered if they had watched me make a fool of myself at the river's edge. They smiled as they had before. They tended the fire, and stood watch just as before. If they had seen what just happened, they never showed it.

The Lord finally broke the silence with a reassuring smile.

"Everyone wants to be free from their Egypt. But few want to be delivered from their wilderness."

I looked at Him a bit puzzled.

"I don't get it. Why would we want to be set free from Egypt but then want to stay in the wilderness?"

"The Egyptians were hard taskmasters, just like sin is to you. The worst of everyone's imagination is fulfilled in Egypt...the worst of everyone's fears and sorrows. No one wants to spend their lives as a slave either of Egypt or of sin. Israel was whipped, beaten, overworked, and underfed. They had their children taken, and their God mocked. They lived as rats in the street. They were robbed of their dignity, their self-respect, and their future. Their lives meant less than nothing to their Egyptian masters.

"Sin does the same thing to you," the Lord continued. "Its temptation whips and beats you to submission. Sin has no respect for your future, your family, or your dignity. It mocks your God, driving you to bow to it. Your life means less than nothing to it. Its only goal is its own gratification. Who would not want to be free from that?"

"Well," I responded, "when You say it like that, I understand. No wonder the Bible says that Israel fled from Egypt. I would, too."

"And you did!" the Lord replied, clearly happy that I understood. "You fled from your own Egypt, your own bondage."

"So now what is the problem?" I asked innocently.

"The problem is that you left what you openly hated and despised when you went out from Egypt, but now you must leave what you secretly love, what you secretly crave, in order to enter the Promised Land."

"But I thought they did not enter because of unbelief."

"That is right," the Lord nodded. "They did not believe that they could live joyfully fulfilled lives without the things they had hidden in their hearts. Those are the true crutches in a person's life."

Chapter Five

The Lord paused for a moment, looking at my perplexed countenance.

"Think about it," He started over. "Who thinks they can live without their favorite fleshly response?"

"Their *favorite* fleshly response?" I protested.

"Of course. That is why it is hard to move beyond the things you love. Everyone wanted to give up making bricks, but who wanted to give up free food and water in the wilderness? Everyone wanted to be able to worship God, but who wanted to risk their lives obeying God?"

My thoughts wandered back to my own past. "We all wanted to be free from drugs, but who wants to be free from gossip or lying or lust or envy? We all wanted to have our lives changed, but not so far as to give up anger or bitterness or revenge."

By now I was beginning to understand.

"You must believe Me when I say that My way is best for you. You must believe Me when I say that there is a much better way than the ways of the wilderness. If you decide to be satisfied with wilderness life, you will never experience the ecstasy of union with your Creator or the wonder of living the dreams He has dreamed for you."

Deep inside I knew He was right. I was afraid to admit it, though. That might mean He would expect me to change all at once. Again, I understood what He meant. It is only the beginning to give Him my heart. He really wants my will.

Even as this argument raged within me, I could feel the tugging of His love and the gentle whisper of His voice. How sweet. How wonderful His Presence! But how could I risk everything I had?

"And what do you have, My son? What do you have now that would be a worthy substitute for all I have for you?"

I did not know why, but I could not give Him an answer.

"My son, I want to take you somewhere. I want to take you to another time, another dimension. I want you to see what unbelief can do to stop My plan for an entire nation."

Before I could protest, we were gone.

Chapter Six

I have no idea how we got from a forested riverside with ministering angels, cool shade, and a soft grassy bed under a mighty tree to this god-forsaken desert. But here we stood. The brightness blinded me for a few moments, but soon I was able to see far more than I wanted to see.

"Walk with Me, My son."

"But where are we?" I hesitated.

"We are in a place of unbelief. We are among those who have fallen short of the glory I had intended for them."

The Lord stood silently for a moment. Tears began to fall freely from His eyes as He began to walk. No one noticed as He moved among them, occasionally stopping to lay His hand on someone or to whisper into someone's ear.

"This is a place of unbelief?" I asked. "What place is it? If they are living in unbelief, why are You praying for them and encouraging them?"

The Lord rose to His feet from the child He was praying for and turned to me. "Because they are Mine," was His passionate reply. "They are My people, and I love them. I could never leave them.

"How can you look upon them with disdain?" the Lord asked me. "You struggle with your decision to go on. I am not giving up on you. I love you."

He looked at me with such compassion, such assurance. "They will respond to Me, just as you will, if, indeed, you want to live in My glory."

I fell to the Lord's feet as the thought of falling short of His glory raced through my heart.

"Forgive me, Lord. I do not want to miss Your best for me. I do not want to fall short of Your dreams for me."

The Lord laid His hand upon me as power flowed into my heart. "Thank You for Your patience, Lord. Please do not give up on me!" With that prayer, the Lord laughed out loud.

"Give up on you? Did you say, 'give up on you'? How can I ever forget the one I nurture at My breast? How can one stop breathing yet continue to live? No, My son, do not worry about that. Forgetting My children is something I can never do."

Overflowing with gratitude and thankfulness, we continued to walk among the children of Israel.

The heat was searing. The sun's rays pounded relentlessly and mercilessly on the barren land and upon the hundreds of thousands of people who camped in this wasted, howling wilderness. They huddled under a huge cloud that engulfed the tiny ridge where they had set up the camp. They ate bread from simple clay pots that they had formed with their hands and then baked in the sweltering sun.

The multitudes sat silently as they ate. They were careful to collect all the crumbs they would need for the day. There were many children to feed, and although they had never run out, they had to make sure they had enough for their evening meal. There would be no more bread from where that came from for the rest of the day.

Smoke from hundreds of fires rose lazily all over the camp. The air was so heavy with heat, though, that the smoke seemed to force itself to rise at all.

Soon the men pulled meat from the fires and began to distribute it among the people. Children fought for the biggest piece as tiny infants screamed in discomfort. Flies swarmed over the meat as hungrily as the children.

Blowing sand and smoke made it almost impossible to breathe. The hot sand burned their eyes so badly that everything around them was nothing more than a blur. Not that there was anything to see, mind you, for as far as the eye could see in any direction, there was nothing but wilderness. Even their tracks behind them were covered by the winds that blew over the sand.

As we walked among these people, I was glad they were not aware we were there. I don't quite know what I would have said to them anyway. They seemed so out of place, so out of touch with reality. They talked like normal people; they acted like normal people; they did all the things normal people usually do—except these people didn't belong there. They were not normal people. They were God's people. They were never meant to suffer so!

The Lord had prepared a way for them that would take them to the land He had promised to them many years ago.

But alas, they were setting the pattern of response that all mankind would follow in the millennia to come. It was a pattern of disobedience and rebellion deeply rooted in the fallacy that they knew better than God Himself.

Now they would pay for that rebellious sin. Not that God was punishing them; they were simply reaping the fruit of following their own opinions rather than believing their Lord. But they were still God's special treasure, and obedient or not, He would take care of them.

He gave them manna for their bread and quail for their meat. He gave them a Rock to follow them that poured out fresh water for all to drink. Their children's clothes grew as the children grew. Their clothes and their shoes never wore out.

The Lord looked at me from a distance as these thoughts passed through my mind. I had forgotten that He knows what I am thinking. The Lord began walking slowly in my direction. I knew what He was going to say.

I was ashamed of myself. Again, I could see myself as I watched these folks. The Lord had made a way for me. He had dreams for me that no man could imagine; yet, I refused. Yes, maybe I thought I knew better, but more likely was the fact that I was just plain afraid. I just did not know for sure that life with Him, life obedient to Him, would be better than what I had. I had to admit it. I liked venting my anger. I enjoyed pouting. There were many useful vices that were handy tools in the right situations. I would have to say "no" to all of them. But what if God did not come through for me? Then what?

I was just afraid to say "yes". I also had to admit that I realized how I, too, presume upon His greatness toward me and His never-ending, never-tiring, and shall I say, ever-prevailing grace toward me.

Like Israel, I am not satisfied with just getting my own way; I want God to bless my plan, and I want Him to pay the tab as well. I want His total approval of my high-minded stubbornness, and I expect Him to see it my way and bless me accordingly. Oh, the patience and mercy of God!

By the time the Lord had come to where I stood, I had fallen to my knees once again to repent of my own unbelief. Whether expressed as fear or rebellion or haughty pride, my unbelief kept me in my own wilderness just as Israel was in theirs.

So, like me, Israel lingered in the wilderness year after year because of their own stubbornness and unbelief. Yet, God took care of them. The truth of this is far more than our religious minds can handle. With most of them, God was not pleased, yet He cared for them because they were His own. He loved them. He desired them. The legal, condemning hand of religion will never understand such powerful and unconditional love. That is, of course, until they see themselves for who they really are without Him, and cry out for mercy as so many others have done. You can always recognize the religious, you know; they are the ones who always accuse, always condemn, and rarely forgive. They have not experienced the incredible forgiving power of the Lord and are jealous of those who have.

So then, how do I experience the provision of the Lord and still understand His will for me? Like Israel of old, it appeared as though I had some relearning to do. I had always been positive that living in the blessing of God meant both that He was pleased with me and that I was in His will.

But looking more closely at Israel, I saw that such was not the case. The Lord was not pleased with them, yet He blessed them because He loved them and was committed to their well-being. It was not because they were obedient to Him, since, of course, they were not.

He began to explain softly to me as we walked, undetected, among His people Israel, "My blessings in your life should never be the way you determine whether or not you are in My will. I take care of you because I love you. As your loving Father, I am committed to your well-being.

"My plan for your life will often take you into circumstances that you might not consider to be such a blessing. In fact, My will may someday lead you to give up your life for My sake.

"Will that be a sign that you are not in My will? I think not. But you must renew your mind to see as I see. I treat you as a mature son. You may often go into battle and fight in circumstances that defy your definitions and your limited understanding."

I could not help thinking of the raging river as He spoke.

"My ways are higher than your ways, and My thoughts are higher than yours. Simply say 'yes' and you will find yourself in the center of My purposes for you, regardless of the circumstances around you."

I was so embarrassed. I always put man's fickle emotions on the Lord, as though He changes His mind about me according to my sins and failures. If I haven't sinned today, God is happy with me. But if I have failed, He is angry with me. How foolish! I serve a God far more loving and merciful than that.

He sees the possibilities within me. I barely see what is just in front of me.

He sees His eternal plan while I see my temporary failures.

He sees His Glory flowing through me while I see my struggling humanity.

Chapter Six

He watches me from the timelessness of eternity while I stubbornly cling to the dimension that threatens my very soul.

"O God, help me to learn from the plight of ancient Israel but not to judge her. For she is a mirror through which I will undoubtedly see myself.

"O God, help me to see as You see, to live where You live, to love as You love."

"O God, help me to let go of the security of my false, fleshly anchors, for they also inherently carry the poison of satan's worst lies."

So my Lord's love is steady, or shall I say, "predictable"? He will always be compassionate, always loving, always forgiving. He cares for me even when I do not deserve to be cared for and provides for me even when I go astray.

I always wondered why God would bless me even when I sinned. I actually wondered sometimes if there was a chance He had missed a sin because His blessing continued to be so profound, so unhindered. Hah! Not a chance. He sees, I am sure of it. He sees and He blesses because we are His children. He still loves us whether we sin or not.

"But, Lord," I asked Him, shaking my head a bit incredulously, "don't You punish us when we sin? I mean, it only makes sense that You would, right?"

The Lord looked at me with half a smile. "I think sin itself eventually does an adequate job of punishment... Do you not agree?"

His response made me shiver. "Is that a good thing or a bad thing?" I mumbled to myself as I quickly walked away. "All this time I thought I was getting away with something."

"You are," my Lord spoke from a distance. I froze where I stood and turned to Him. He continued, "The punishment due you is still due someone…Me. You are why I took the cross, to take the punishment that rightfully belongs to you. Have you never read, 'He always lives to make intercession for the saints'? Every time you sin, the punishment falls on Me so My Father's blessing can fall on you.

"No, My son, We are not about punishment; We are about wholeness—wholeness and relationship. Sin itself takes care of the punishment."

I was stunned. Never before had I heard such a thing. Such love! Such mercy! Such desire for the likes of me. It was certain that I had no idea of the depths that would move God to such love. I had no idea who I was or the fellowship my Lord was calling me to.

Such, too, was the lot of this people of God, this Israel whom the prophets had said walked in the anointing and power of Jehovah Himself. But they looked just like me. They did not seem to act much like they belonged to any god at all, let alone the great and mighty Jehovah. Nonetheless, His compassion for them would never wane; His mercy toward them would not come to an end.

They were tired and discouraged. They had followed that cloud and that fire, but where had it gotten them? They were still in the wilderness, still far from the promise they had clearly received from the Lord, still clueless that their unbelief had sentenced them to wander in the loneliness of this forsaken wasteland. Their children were being born as nomads and their parents were dying off every day, being returned to the earth in graves that were soon consumed by the desert itself—graves that would never be found again.

Tempers were short as they recounted the early days of their deliverance. To be sure, most were no longer too certain that it was deliverance after all.

They ate the food of angels as bitterness grew in their hearts.

Israel gathered bread and meat miraculously provided by their Lord, yet there was no gratefulness in their hearts. The roar of the mighty river of water gushing out from a huge Rock to the rear of the camp seemed to plead with them to remember the promise and urge them to embrace their hope.

But they had no hope. Their own stubbornness had seen to that. They had no destination. It was so clear. Oh, I know you will try to correct me. I know you will tell me that they indeed had a great destination. But quite honestly, look carefully into their eyes. What do you see? Or more correctly, what don't you see?

The people talked of a Promised Land that God had assured them was theirs. They spoke of a land that was flowing with milk and honey...over there...somewhere. God had said He would surely lead them into a land of their own, a land where they would prosper and be the envy of the neighborhood. But alas, that promise seemed so far away today, so far away.

I stopped in front of an older woman whose face bore the scars of years of struggle and prayer. Her straggling gray hair, matted by dust and sweat, lay tight against her drawn and grooved face. As I peered into her deep brown eyes, I could see into the depths of her heart.

Only the dim flicker of a candle continued to burn there. Surrounded by cobwebs and mildew, the tiny light struggled to burn. The wax, all but gone, caused the flame to fight for its very life, as though with its demise, the candle of life itself would also die.

Off in the far corner of this old woman's heart, a small but menacing devil hid in the shadows. I recognized it immediately, not because of some great gift of discernment, but because I had fought this demon more times than I care to remember. It was the demon that kept me from responding to my Lord when He brought me into the river. It was unbelief! That same sinister force had sidetracked the entire nation of Israel. It had drawn God's people away from their highest purposes. But unbelief seems to be such a little thing. It is hard to imagine how it could have had such an effect on so many people. But the proof was there. Israel was caught, trapped between bondage and God's promises.

Like so many of us, they knew better than to actually go back to Egypt. But they also did not want to go forward, risking everything they had, as though they had anything worth keeping as they wandered aimlessly and hopelessly in the wilderness. They had become content where they were, short of God's promise for them.

This woman and her people had learned to live in the wilderness. Well, not really live. They learned to survive there, as most of us learn to survive short of God's glory. It was actually much safer than the Promised Land. They always knew what to expect here in the wilderness. They knew there would be food and water. They had learned how to gather the manna and the quail. They knew how to get water as it poured as a mighty river from the Rock.

But as for the Promised Land, they didn't know for sure what would be there. They only knew what the Lord told them would be there. But deep down in their hearts, they were just not sure of His promises. The wilderness may not be God's plan, but it was certainly safer and it was still better than living in Egypt.

"Quite different when you look at them from the outside," the Lord said to me.

"I guess the same could be said of me," I nodded. The Lord just smiled.

"It is as though they developed their own theology of poverty. I guess they had to do something to help make the wilderness more tolerable," I philosophized. "It was okay to be poor. God loved the poor and would do marvelous things for them. Even the Word says the poor will always be among us. That most certainly meant us, right?"

"It is never holy to be in want," the Lord interrupted me. "They had forgotten that the wealth of the heathen is laid up for the righteous."

Oh my, how they sound like us! In our righteous rejection of contemporary doctrines of opulence, I fear we have used that as our opportunity to settle for far less than He would provide.

Incredible. Our righteous response to false doctrine has turned into a self-righteous excuse for living far below God's blessing.

Nonetheless, these issues still only sidetrack us from God's desire for union with Him. Somewhere, in this life, on this planet, He will have a people who care nothing for the things that perish. They truly will seek first His Kingdom and the King who reigns there, knowing confidently that absolutely everything else will be cared for by Him. They will know His voice and will walk humbly, quietly, doing the will of God.

But just like us, Israel's doctrines of spiritual contentment (which only thinly veil their unbelief) imprisoned them short of God's glory. For when one chooses to camp, one must justify the encampment. Thus the doctrine that made them content with their lot in life...er...their spiritual achievements, had to be developed. They decided that the miraculous had to be a sure sign that they were in the center of God's will. Maybe the Promised Land was to be for the next generation after all, or maybe even the real good promises are for Heaven.

Soon the encampments would have turned into permanent towns and cities, had it not been for the pillar of smoke and the pillar of fire that annoyingly moved every time that they had settled into a somewhat comfortable routine.

How frustrating it was for the fleshly side of humanity! No sooner had they pitched their tents, had their fires built, and had all the rocks cleared out from under their beds, then it was time to move on again.

How foolish for them to decide to stay in camp when the Presence moved on.

How foolish, indeed.

Would to God that we had a pillar of smoke and a pillar of fire to keep us from "denominationalizing" every time God did something wonderful for a group of people.

Would to God we could discern such movements of the Spirit today. Instead, the cloud of His Presence is dismissed as fleshly emotions and the fire of God as demonic or, at best, mere human dissatisfaction.

We hold on to what has been, even at the risk of what should be.

We allow ourselves to be frightened away from His glory by small people who have never seen His glory or experienced the vibrant interactive power of the living God. These guys sit in tiny studios pronouncing carnal edicts and frightful accusations, blindly judging what they know nothing about. Planting uncertainty into the hearts of seeking believers, these religious bounty hunters are nothing more than self-appointed keepers of their own unholy grail. They do not enter His Presence themselves, and they prevent others from entering as well.

God have mercy on their souls.

But there was a side to the wilderness that the people could not see. Certainly, in the wilderness, their daily food was provided. But also in the wilderness, they would never accumulate wealth. Water gushed out of a Rock for them to drink, but they would never build cities or even homes of their own. Their clothes grew with the children and never wore out, but the wilderness offered no future and nothing to pass on to the generations to come.

There would never be any security there, either. Without question, they would never please God in the wilderness, for He had destined them to go on into the Promised Land, the place of union with God. If they didn't possess the Land, they would most certainly fall short of the glory of God.

Their unbelief would condemn them to a death never intended by their loving Lord and rob them and their children of the glorious liberty and power the Promised Land offered them.

But those grand promises were probably for the millennium anyway. Right?

Nonetheless, I could not judge them too harshly, for they reminded me of myself. I am haunted by His word that ever beckons me forward. My own doctrines of contentment cause me, too, to fall pitifully short of His glory. I, too, have mistaken God's supernatural provision for His approval. I have become satisfied with looking upon Him from a distance, when all He really wants is true and genuine interactive fellowship with me. I have accepted confusion and uncertainty as a way of life, somehow convincing myself that that is God's plan instead of a signal that something is very wrong. So I develop doctrines that insist that confusion and poverty are the way things are supposed to be. I settle for life in a wilderness full of shadows and emptiness, having become certain that this is His plan, that this is the most I can expect. All the while I ignore His burning Spirit within my heart to go on into the Promised Land, the Most Holy Place, where union with Him is a way of life. I have become content with wilderness life, having become too fearful of what anything more than that may cost me.

Chapter Six

So in my self-righteous unbelief, I miss His plan. More tragically, I miss genuine interactive fellowship with the living God, selling my birthright for a bowl of porridge.

My stomach is full but my heart languishes.

My flesh is safe but my destiny is just beyond my reach.

My doctrines are secure but my future has been sacrificed.

I was stunned as I backed away from this tired Israelite. She had fallen short of His glory. These people lived in the daily experience of His miracle wonders. He supernaturally supplied everything they would ever need. They were people of His Presence. He was in their midst, leading and comforting them by day and by night. But they fell short of His glory. They fell short of His dream for them.

They would never realize what they had sacrificed in allowing unbelief to rule them. They would never understand that God had so much more for them. They were content to live where they were, short of the Promised Land, short of union with their Creator.

Even though they spoke with such clarity and could recount every promise with exacting detail—even though they could tell their story with great passion and conviction—they were still in the wilderness!

They had begun as sojourners, following their Lord in search of the Promised Land, but they had become nomads with no destination, no land of their own, and no future.

Weeping in repentance, I asked the Lord not to leave me in my unbelief. I began to realize that being blessed by the Lord did not really satisfy the hunger in my soul. As much as I love blessings, there is something eternal, something more beautiful, something more fulfilling than anything this earthy realm can deliver. I must have His Presence. Only His Presence satisfies the ravenous thirst of my soul. And I really mean His genuine Presence—the Presence that I can feel, and I can touch.

I always thought it was a sin to have an unfulfilled yearning for Him even though He had blessed me. But now I understand. Gifts will never satisfy. Answered prayer does not even satisfy. I was made to be one with Him. I was made to joyfully, eagerly respond to His voice, doing His will because it pleases Him, because nothing takes the place of the thrill of obeying His voice.

"O Lord, I never want to just work for You again, hoping that somehow You will bless my efforts. I want to walk in Your dreams for me. I want to worship You with my obedience, to hear the sound of Your voice deep in my spirit."

As I repented before my Lord, He gathered me into His arms and said so softly, "All have sinned and have come short of the glory of God. But with My grace, you can be certain that you will not come short of it." Suddenly that Scripture, which for so long had been neatly tucked away for a sinner's prayer, became alive again.

I now realized that it was my responsibility to say "yes" to Him every day. He would use the person who had learned simply to respond to Him. He was always wooing, always calling, relentlessly striving with me. I needed only say "yes".

I found myself interceding on my own behalf, as well as on the behalf of the countless millions who might go to their graves never knowing why they were born.

"Be careful," the voice of the Lord came tenderly and softly, as I prayed, "that *you* do not come short of the glory of God."

Section Two

Chapter Seven

As quickly as we were whisked off to the wilderness, we were back in the security of the little clearing beside the river. Well, I was back at the clearing. The fire still crackled and the angels still stood guard. The Lord, however, was not there. Nonetheless, the sense of His Presence was still so sweet.

It seemed as though He was giving me some time to think about what had just happened. I had no idea of the passing of time, though. It was so strange. It was as though I was lifted out of time and into a dimension where time served rather than ruled. It was a dimension where my five senses could not adequately discern the environment around me, which meant I had little clue as to what was happening. I quickly learned, however, to stretch my spirit and to listen carefully to it. In this dimension, my spirit seemed to be more at home than my body.

Consequently, time and the feelings associated to its passing were a mystery. I have no idea how long I was at the river's edge, or whether it even mattered. I was so used to being a slave to time that this notion of time as a servant was definitely new to me.

Whether in time or out of time, I reviewed the visit to the wilderness again and again. The last thing I wanted to do was to lose the sense of hope and possibilities I had had as I walked with the Lord and was instructed by Him.

Eventually the memories faded and the sense of His Presence waned, even though I sat in the presence of angels and His supernatural provision. I had not moved from this comfortable place He had carried me to by His tender love and gentle mercies. But something was definitely changing. It seemed that the longer I was away from His Manifest Presence, the less I anticipated His appearing in me. I do not know how it happened, but I soon realized that all I had were memories.

Yes, I was safe. Yes, I was cared for. Of course, I had everything I needed to survive, but I was still on the wrong side of the river, the wrong side of my humanity. Though in the presence of angels, I was still guarding my own life, making my own decisions, planning my own future. I was too frightened to respond to His repeated calls to me. Oh, yes, did I forget to tell you that? All the while I was enjoying the place where He had brought me, He was calling me to come to Him, singing the wonderful songs of Zion, the songs of His Presence, the songs of union with Him. But I was unwilling to trust Him, to believe Him, to move beyond the security He had provided.

So here I was, totally cared for, but far from who I was born to be, entertaining myself with memories from wonderful experiences with my Lord—memories that were now fading away. The clearing, once a place of joyful anticipation, had become a place of lonely dullness, holding only the memory of where I said "no" to my Lord. Try as I may to ignore it and cover it with a barrage of very important religious activities, I knew, if no one else did, that this is where I had stopped. This is where I had decided to camp. I would be here, in the wilderness, within sight of my destiny, for the remainder of my life. I had said "yes" with my desire, but I could not respond with my will. I was alone once again.

I finally had to admit what I had tried to ignore. There was really no other choice. I had stopped short of my destiny. I had gotten sidetracked and had become busy with so many immensely important things. From dawn to far after dusk I was consumed with peripheral and sidetracking issues, all the while trying desperately to convince myself that everything was fine, that all these things I was doing were making a difference. But now I can admit it. Granted, it might be too late, but I can admit it. I stopped. I simply stopped. And now here I sit, on the wrong side of my dreams. In stunned silence, I watched the days flow quickly by. Time was ruling again—and moving most swiftly. To be sure, there were meager attempts to recapture time, to make it a servant once again, but it was to no avail. A day lost is a day lost, only to be recovered in another dimension, if I could ever allow myself to live there.

Some days, the pain was particularly tough to handle. Some days I didn't want to wake up. For God was not the only One who knew I had stopped. The enemies of my soul were thrilled with my plight, with my decision—or indecision, as it were...

Their sounds torment me day and night. Their heckling voices from far across the water, that hideous, mocking sound, constantly rob me of precious and elusive sleep. They are always there reminding me, always taunting me. On calm days, when the wind is quiet, their sounds seem to be louder than the river itself.

Their fires burn high and bright throughout the night. They are just close enough to cast faint shadows that seem to dance with the flames on the shore. Their songs and evil merriment pierce any sliver of hope that dares creep back into my heart. They have won. It is plain and simple. They dance a morbid dance on ground God promised to me—land filled with milk and honey, land that builds wealth and plants hope deep in the heart.

They are dancing on my destiny and gloating over my unbelief.

The worst part of all, though, is when they see me watching them. I hate when that happens! Their songs get a little louder, their dance a little faster. They flex their muscles and growl with hideous mocking. They jeer and gesture at me with merciless sarcasm and hate. If I never see them or hear them again, I am afraid it will not matter, for their images and their badgering is forever etched in my mind and on my heart.

Like angry, spoiled children, they taint my hope with lies and torment. Their ugly graffiti covers my heart, upon which was etched His love and promises to me, obscures God's words and steals my hope. They are dancing on my land; they are destroying and defacing my heart, a heart which long ago was laid bare before the King alone to carefully and lovingly write His laws.

I wonder if there is indeed any hope at all, for my enemies have so defaced and so ruthlessly tried to erase these words that I have clung to and trusted in so desperately. But now I am only broken…broken and tired.

His Kingdom has not come, at least not to me, and my heart is no longer the beacon of hope and direction it once was. Now it barely resembles a heart at all. It only exists with scattered and painful beats. And if the truth be really known, it only continues to beat regretfully. For I should be most relieved at this point if it would not continue to beat at all.

But this night was a night that would not grant the relief of real sleep, but only restless and tormenting naps filled with the dreams of what could have been. If I had only said "yes" to Him as He called out to me with wonderful songs of love and desire. But now I have said "no" so often that I have forgotten the exhilaration of the sound of His voice and the anticipation of the joy that obedience to His Voice never fails to give.

Memories flood my mind of days of abandoned trust in my Lord. I leaped at His command and found my greatest fulfillment and joy in simply doing His will. They were marvelous days indeed. Nothing could go wrong, nothing could stop me. Nothing, that is, until I came to this wretched riverbank. Oh, I always knew it was there, but somehow I was always able to avoid it, to steer my path away from it. There had been times that were so good I almost convinced myself that the river did not exist and that the enemies lurking on the other side were merely figments of my overactive imagination.

"Surely, this is my destiny," I would proclaim triumphantly to myself. "Surely I have come to life's greatest fulfillment."

But alas, God, in His infinite patience and mercy, knew that my destiny lay far beyond the borders of a wilderness filled with dusty uncertainty and crippling unbelief. In His mercy, He would lead me to where I did not want to be: face to face with the enemies of my soul. Face to face with what would forever rob me of that for which I was born: to love my Lord and to be found one with Him in thought, desire, love, and compassion. He would bring me to the edge of my humanity, where all the rules changed and all my human strengths were brought to naught. He would bring me to the edge of my destiny, where only He can be trusted, even above my own reason and intellect. If I would live when I faced these guys, I would live because I was hidden in Christ, covered in the shadow of His wings.

But nonetheless, here I lay, on a cold and rocky riverside far from sleep and definitely far from hope. As I lay in the morning chill, I could see their fires, watch the silhouettes of their delirious dancing, and hear their songs of apparent victory over my life.

I had become way too familiar with these enemies. They were all too easily recognizable and predictable. Just when it would seem they were gone, I knew they would return with hateful fury. They always seemed to know when the King was beckoning me to cross the river and stake a claim in my land. Several times I nearly stepped into the water; that is, until these enemies gathered on the far shore, jeering, threatening, and angrily accusing me. All the while I stood listening, forgetting that my humanity did not disqualify me, but would be the very means with which God would show the world His glory.

But knowing that did not always help during the battle. These enemies were always so convincing! They always seemed to know my deepest secrets and fears. I am quite sure that no one knew where they came from, but Bitterness, Unworthiness, and Sorrow always seemed to find precisely the right Fear that I dreaded the most at that moment. They would find them somewhere and arrogantly parade them in front of me with scandalous shamelessness.

These guys always sent chills up my spine. I watched them squat on my land, preventing me from crossing the waters of my humanity; preventing me from trusting Him who beckons me to live beyond myself, beyond the rushing and turbulent waters of my own self-centered desires, into the dreams He has always dreamed for me.

Chapter Eight

Sometime during my stay beneath the protection of this mighty tree and the angels who stayed with me, my heart began to ache. It was a small ache at first, easy to ignore. But it grew steadily. I did not realize I was trying to drown it out and cover it with other things, but I was. Nonetheless, it continued to grow until I just could not ignore it any longer.

I turned my head to look to the river. To my surprise, the landscape had changed dramatically. The tree was now just on the edge of the water, not the long walk it had been before. The soft grass of the clearing was gone. The fire was gone, as were the angels who tended it. I looked away from the river to discover that the clearing itself was now gone. The treeless land stretched for as far as I could see. Low brush and swirling dust were all that remained of my precious world, my peaceful clearing.

The only constant was the churning angry waters of the river that continued to defy my love, my faith, and my future.

Somehow, I was not surprised at the change of the landscape. I guess deep inside I was expecting it. The Lord said He would never leave me or give up on me. I knew this was His doing to get my attention.

It worked.

The aching within for Him was now the ruling force of my life. I thought of my Lord constantly, often thinking of His warm embrace and His healing touch.

Oh, how I loved Him! How I longed for Him. I remembered my prayer to Him. I still meant every word of it…every word.

"Jesus, I give You my heart. I really do."

But I have come to understand that His Kingdom comes when He has my will as well as my heart. They do not independently possess the power of His Kingdom. It is true that I must "be" before I can "do". It is also true that many try to "do" without "being". That has little hope of working either. But at some point, if His Kingdom is to be seen on this planet, the "being in Him" and the "doing His will" must come together in joyful harmony within me.

"Lord, I ache inside. I ache for You, to be with You, to please You."

I sat silently on the side of the river, peering with great longing into the future, into my future. I remember seeing my Lord call to me from that shore. The hot wind made it difficult to see it now. The wind drove dust into my face, stinging my eyes as they were bombarded with grains of sand. It felt as though the sun was baking rivulets of tears deep into my reddened, sunken cheeks.

The heat was searing.

The sun's rays pounded relentlessly and mercilessly on the barren land.

Blowing sand and dust made it almost impossible to breathe. The combination of the two burned so badly that everything was merely a blur. Not that there was anything to see, mind you, for as far as the eye could look in any direction, there was nothing but wilderness.

Then, in absolute shock, I leaped to my feet. I could not believe what I was seeing. There, far into the wilderness, rose the smoke of thousands of fires. The smell of burnt meat, mingled with smoke and dust, filled the air. I heard the faint bleating of sheep over the howl of the wind, and the cry of children could faintly be heard.

"This cannot be happening. This has got to be a dream."

I turned around to see that the tree I had rested under and that had often comforted me was now nothing more than a large insect-infested stump rising only inches higher than I stood.

"Everything is gone!"

I turned again to the depths of the wilderness to see if my eyes really were seeing what I thought they were seeing.

"The sun. The sun is playing tricks on me. I am sure of it!"

"Now you are in the wilderness with everyone else!" A heckling voice shouted from behind me. It was Fear. I could recognize him anywhere. "Now you have no place to go!"

He was right. Now I was stuck in the wilderness too, probably forever!

Then Regret called to me. "You should have said 'yes' when you had the chance. Now you are finished! You are finished!"

I turned wildly to look across the river.

I could see them. Shielding my eyes from the blinding sun, they were barely visible, far in the distance, on the other side of the river, dancing and mocking my struggle. It was no accident that they were standing just where the Lord had stood with His arms open to me, calling me to Himself.

"You were with your Lord just a little while ago, and already you are shaking with fear. You will never make it!" the Accuser shouted quite truthfully.

Over the noise of the rushing river and the relentless blowing of the wind, their laughter and mocking continued. I wanted to return their arguments. But my head ached, and my heart was suffering far more deeply.

"Why am I listening to them?" I asked myself. But this time I would have to listen to their taunting. The day had been much too hot and much too depressing, and I did not have the strength to fight. The past made me weary just thinking about it, let alone arguing about it. I know the regret. I know the opportunity I missed. I should have just said "yes". At least I would be there now.

Lost in my own self-pity and regret, I was stunned at the familiar feeling of a gentle, loving hand on my shoulder.

"Lord!" I jumped to my feet and wrapped my arms around Him. "You are back! You came back!"

I could feel the smile on His face. "I never left, My son. I never left."

"But look at our clearing. While You were gone, everything changed. The angels are gone. The fire is gone. The grass is gone. Everything is like a wilderness! And the time! Where did the time go? All the dreams You had for me are gone. Lord, everything is gone!"

Chapter Eight

The Lord laughed out loud as He embraced me. "Nothing is gone. You have simply lost your sight for things eternal. Everything is as it was, for it is still now."

There is no way I understood what He had just said, but I was just so glad He was with me again. "Lord, please do not leave me again. Please stay with me."

The Lord sighed as He kissed my cheek. "I will always be with you. You must see, My son, that your view changed. I was always here; My Presence has been always near to you."

"Oh, Lord! Please forgive me, but I do not want to talk right now. I just want You to hold me."

And so He did.

For minutes, for hours, in time or out of time...who knew? Who cared? The power of His love engulfed me. I could sense Him deep within my heart. His Spirit bore witness to my spirit, melting my frustration, my fear. And yes, even my will began to melt into His. Everything within me was saying "yes" to Him. I drifted in and out of time as He changed my thoughts and my desires and filled me with Himself. I knew that He had not gone away; He was always there, waiting for me, praying for me, believing in me to respond to the ache that He had placed within me.

Chapter Nine

J awoke to find myself alone on the riverbank, save that once again the sweetness of His Presence, something I had not experienced for a long, long time, still lingered. Deep inside, I knew that I was ready to give my will over to Him. I knew He would soon call my name and I would have to cross the river. But I also knew He would be with me.

As night fell, I struggled with the uncertainty of what life would be like without my fleshly escapes and crutches. I had always relied on them, but only in times of complete desperation, of course. Now it was certain that I could not rely on them at all. I would have to trust the Lord and live in the "yes" of my God instead of in the hiding places that only brought more trouble than I could handle.

These thoughts made this night a fitful night, a particularly agitating night. In fact, it was a night like I had not experienced in a long while. I argued with myself and satan. Okay, it was not satan's fault. It was my fault. I was the one who had to decide. The argument was really with myself as I struggled to let go of the things I secretly loved and believed I needed so badly.

Had I not been so desperately lost in my own misery, I would have recognized that this was a very different night indeed. I did not understand that, one way or another, this would be my last night on the wretched riverbank.

I tossed and turned, looking for a comfortable spot. You might be thinking that after so many years on the same bank, I could have done something to make it more comfortable. But alas, riverbanks are not for resting; their purpose is not for living. Despite numerous attempts over the years, it was impossible to become comfortable there.

As I turned over for what seemed to be the thousandth time, I got a glimpse of something on the far shore. It moved so quickly...there, there it was again! And again! When I jumped to my feet, I made out a form of something pacing back and forth on the other side of the river. It looked directly at me.

An icy chill raced through my body. My heart beat so loudly I was sure it was about to explode. I was waiting for my Lord, but instead, who knew what lurked in the darkness?

Hot and cold flashed alternately and sometimes simultaneously through my body as fear engulfed the depths of my soul. *What new fear is this?* I thought to myself frantically as I stumbled behind a rock to hide. *I have never seen this one!* It paced back and forth, back and forth, always looking at me, always turning its head so as not to lose sight of me. It walked on four legs and was determined with every step. A low, guttural roar arose in the darkness, barely audible over the sound of rushing water, of rushing humanity.

Absolutely without warning, the creature bolted toward the river and leaped toward the bank directly in front of me. With a roar so loud it seemed to crack open the night, it soared effortlessly over the water.

Chapter Nine

The panic within was so intense, I simply could not move. I stood helplessly frozen with terror as it flew toward me. *Here I will die,* I thought as it landed in front of me, its feet sending sand and stone in every direction, its hot breath releasing fresh shock waves of fear through my heart. I cringed as I closed my eyes, feeling its hot breath on my face and waiting for the death blow. Then all was quiet. All was still. I remained frozen with my eyes squeezed shut, still certain that death was imminent, when the familiar hand on my shoulder and a gentle, "Do not be afraid, My son," caused me to melt to the ground.

"Lord!" I could not help but shout. "Did You see that thing? What was it? Is it gone?" I leaped to my feet to embrace Him.

"That was not a thing," the Lord said with a sparkle in His eye. "That was Me."

"That was You? That was You? That was You! Yes, yes, of course! You are the Lion of the tribe of Judah!"

The Lord laughed out loud.

"Lord, don't do that to me! You scared me half… Oh, I am sorry, Lord. I did not mean any disrespect."

"None taken."

"Do You know what You look like jumping over that river? My goodness!"

"I know. I know. I look bad. Bad enough to destroy any of your puny enemies," He said with understandable confidence.

The Lord suddenly turned serious. He took me by the hand and looked intently into my eyes, into the depth of my unbelief. "If you will hear My voice and come to Me, I will make your enemies My enemies; your adversaries will be My adversaries. You shall not fear your enemies, for I will go ahead of you, and they shall be completely destroyed."

It took only moments for me to melt once again, sobbing into His arms. "Forgive my unbelief, forgive my fears. I should have known Your words to me are faithful." The Lord softly spoke, "The words of the Lord are pure words; as silver tried in a furnace on the earth, refined seven times."

"You must think I am such a coward, such a baby. I do not understand how You…" I think the Lord had heard enough. He gently interrupted my hopeless introspection.

"I know exactly who you are, My son. You the son of My affection, the apple of My eye, one in whom I am determined to live and enjoy for all eternity."

Oh. Well. My confidence began to grow as He encouraged me with these words. I lay there quietly praising Him for His grace and His love that had never forgotten me or given up on me.

His Spirit enveloped my spirit.

As He held me, I remembered the first time He brought me to the river's edge. It had been a terrible, humiliating day. My enemies tormented me without mercy as the Lord stepped into the water, still holding onto my hand. How clearly I remember His confident bidding. "I will not leave you," He said with calm assurance. Yet, the blast of those nagging fears over-powered me. I broke free from His grasp and ran from the water's edge. I was so certain that I could not face my fears or any other of my enemies. I knew there was no way to be free of them.

I cannot remember the number of times the Lord returned to me, beckoning me to go on. Yet each time I refused. And each time He left, I cried out with fervent resolve that I would not let it happen again. But it did happen again. And again. And again. The visits from the Lord became less frequent. His times with me were shorter. Of course, He often came at times that were not exactly convenient. I had things to do—things for the Lord. I began to wonder just how many times I could refuse Him until He would not return at all. I guess, if the truth be told, He always came and He always wanted to stay. But I was too involved in work for fellowship, for union.

Oh, but now He is here, I thought to myself. *Now I would not turn Him away again. Now, with my head close to His heart, I knew I was safe. I knew I would go with Him.*

With the sound of His heart beating in my ears and the warmth of His breath on my face, I drifted off to the deepest and most restful sleep I could remember. The Lord smiled as He held me close to Himself.

"It's nearly time to go," the Lord awakened me at first light. Sitting before me were a raisin cake, a piece of meat, and an earthenware cup of wine. "Eat, strengthen yourself. It will be a long day."

The Lord walked back and forth, peering into the Promised Land. He patiently waited while I finished.

"I must go," the Lord said, "but remember, when you hear My voice, do not harden your heart. I am with you, even when you cannot see Me."

Before I could say a word, He leaped over the river and landed on the other side as a majestic lion.

How does He do that? I thought to myself.

With a roar of absolute authority, He disappeared over the horizon. Soon everything was silent again, save the monotonous thunder of the rushing water.

As I sat there in the early morning mist, I could feel the yearning, aching of my heart. Sometimes it burned with desire to please Him. Other times, it ached in want of His love. Still other times it seemed to leap with an unexplainable anticipation of hearing the sound of His voice. However it seemed, it was wonderful to know His love, His friendship, and His plan for my life were all intact and that His intention had not changed, even after all the times I had rejected His Presence.

Suddenly, I could hear the voice of the Lord speaking from deep within my spirit. I could not make out what He said, but I knew the time had come. My heart raced with fear as I stumbled to my feet. I knew there was no turning back. There is nothing back there for me now. For the first time, I really understood that.

I was shocked to discover it was near evening. I had spent the entire day in prayer. But now, with nightfall approaching, I could not understand His leading to cross at such a late hour. I looked into the rushing river. My heart seemed to be pumping blood at the same rate as the flow of the river. I was coming to the end of myself, of my humanity. I looked back at the wilderness that had been my sustenance for so many years. This land was familiar; If there was nothing else there, there was safety. I knew what to expect; I knew what would happen tomorrow, and the next day, and the next, and the next. But it did not have the grip on me it once had. The fire, the provision, the tree that gave me such security—it all meant nothing to me now. I wanted to go with my Lord.

Chapter Ten

The hand of the Lord firmly placed on my shoulder startled me out of deep thought. "Moses is dead," the Lord said. I fell to my knees.

"I do not want to live in a land that is passing away," I responded.

"Moses is dead, My son. Let us arise and cross the river." At that moment He was gone. His words burned inside of me, planting a confidence and assurance in me that I had never had. I arose and looked all around. I determined in myself to be obedient. I arose and began to walk slowly toward the river's edge.

If water could talk, it talked to me that day. With thunderous currents and unforgiving power the water mocked my intentions and raised its roar to deafening heights. "I dare you to defy me!" it echoed in my heart. "Who are you to resist my power and fury?"

I hesitated. I held my breath. "Lord, I need You so soon!"

His arms wrapped me securely from behind. "It is okay; let us cross the river."

I am afraid I have to step in before I can cross, I thought to myself.

"I heard that."

"Oh, yes. I keep forgetting."

We slowly continued to walk down the bank to the water. As my foot slipped into the water, I did not know whether it was warm or cold. I only knew it was mean—mean and angry.

The water swirled around my foot as it searched for the bottom of the river. It was nearly knee-deep. I carefully put my other foot in, cautiously watching for a good landing place. The muddy water seemed to want to swallow me up as it swirled around my legs. Carefully, cautiously, and not too confidently, I went on. Each step brought me to deeper, seemingly angrier water. The grip of the Lord got tighter as we went on. With each step I began to understand that it was not my legs the water really wanted; it was my confidence, my desire, my future, and ultimately my relationship with the One who held me so tightly as we walked.

As I worked my way across, the twilight was shaken with an awful shriek. The Lord tightened His grip. It seemed to be coming from right in front of me. My heart nearly stopped with dread as I looked up to discover my enemies gathering on the shoreline, just as they had done so many times before. Some even ventured into the river. My legs weakened with fear as I saw that angry and hideous horde mocking and jeering my progress. "He trusted the Lord; let Him save him now!" and "He made the Lord his delight; now watch him be humiliated."

I stood in frozen silence. The river was now nearly chest-deep. It raged around me in angry confusion. It was as though the water, too, battled against me, actually conspiring with my enemies. I glanced back to the wilderness. I was still closer to that shore. I could probably make it without a problem. The water seemed to push harder at me, trying to knock me off the tenuous balance I was trying to maintain. Just when I thought I could make it, my deepest, most hidden fear proudly walked onto the beach. I was about to be found out. I was about to be discovered! The very thing I thought was buried so deep that it would never be seen was now staring me directly in my face.

I could no longer feel His arms around me. My heart sank. Every ounce of strength and determination I had was instantly gone. My knees buckled. The river of my humanity was about to win. I was about to be swept away. All my other tormentors seemed to dance merrily around it in a sort of morbid victory dance. Without even thinking, I turned away to head back to the shore from which I had started. Tears streamed from my eyes as I tried to run in this merciless torrent. There was nothing to hold onto, nothing to help me along. I strained for every drop of energy within as I pushed for the shore from which I had come.

Then came a quiet, reassuring voice. "Today, if you hear My voice, do not harden your heart."

I was nearly drowning in my weakness; I certainly did not have the strength to turn toward my destiny once again. I cried out, "Lord, my years are spent and my heart is weak with fear. My tormentors mock me with cruel hatred. There is no help in them. They only want my death."

Again came the voice from within, "Today, if you hear My voice, do not harden your heart." With those words, I kept moving forward into what I knew would be certain death. For there was no strength to go on. No strength to fight.

But He had said enough to stir up a desperate resolve deep inside. With all the strength I could muster, I threw my fists in the air and screamed with all my heart, "NO, NO, no more, not this time!" A surge of hope exploded in my heart. Almost instantly, the water was over my head and my feet were swept from beneath me. The water whipped my head against large stones and dragged me to the bottom where the force of the water smashed my face into the riverbed. With a momentary push to the surface, I gasped quickly for air. My ears were greeted with the sound of my enemies as they shrieked in wild hysteria. They knew that my own humanity was my greatest enemy.

I swam, I gasped for air, I pushed off rocks, I defied the anger of this river, this humanity of mine. I was once and for all as sure I wanted Him as I had ever been. If it cost my life in pursuit of Him, then so be it. I would not turn back.

By now my clothes were mere rags that clung loosely to my body. I was covered with cuts and bruises and nearly delirious from the blows to my head. I sometimes wondered if it was all real, or if it was really a dream. My heart raced wildly, out of control with fear. I wondered who'd get me first, the river or, if perchance I survived its raging torrents, the enemies on the other side.

Just when I was sure I would pass out with utter exhaustion, I realized I was at the river's edge, only to have that realization shattered by the awful presence of my deepest anxieties, sorrows, and pain. I began to drag myself from the water as these lifelong tormentors ran hysterically toward me with their wicked lies and evil temptations. I clung to a rock that stuck out of the mud. My body still partially in the water, I buried my head in my arms, waiting to be consumed by my adversaries. "Into Your hands I commend my spirit," I whispered to the Lord, "for one day in obedience is better than ten thousand living for myself."

Chapter Ten

Suddenly, there was a roar so loud that I slipped off the rock and nearly ended up downstream. The air was filled with confusion and unintelligible screams. I could hear painful moans, flesh ripping, bones cracking, and enemies scattering into the foothills and caves of the Promised Land. "I am the Lord your God who contends for you." The land shook with the sound of His roar.

Suddenly, all was quiet. I was afraid to look up. But then I heard His laughter. I slowly looked up to see one of my enemies lying on the bank of the river.

"You got one?" was all I could seem to ask. "Yes," the Lord said in triumph. "We got one!"

As I pulled myself on shore, I could see the mangled carcass of my most dreaded fear. I cried with endless tears of gratitude. "This one won't bother you again," He said. "Shall we bury it?" I queried rather foolishly. "Nay," the Lord said, "leave him for the buzzards. That way there will be no trace of him, and no place to come back and find him."

The Lord then turned to me and said quite solemnly, "Remember this day, and what I have done for you. Be strong and courageous; possess the land, and I will cause your enemies to fear you as you have feared them, and I will drive them out before you.

"Call upon Me, and I will answer you. I am with you all the time, especially when you cannot see Me."

As He turned to go, I realized that my heart still ached. After all that I had been through, I had fully expected my heart to be at rest. But it was worse than ever. I ached for His Presence; my heart burned for His nearness. It was a sweet, yet painful burning within the deepest part of my being.

I was so certain, so sure that it would be released once I crossed the river. But it remained the central driving force of my life. It consumed everything about me. I could not think; I could barely work. At times it was a trial to do even the most simple things. I could not bring myself even to do many of the things that had brought me close to the Lord in times past. So much of what I did and who I was seemed so unimportant, so shallow.

Now I really began to wonder if there was something wrong with me. "Do other people feel this way? Do others have this panting of their souls for the Lord? Are there some, like me, who have tried to quell the yearning of the Spirit? Am I doomed to try to deal with this for the rest of my life?"

I had spent many years not understanding the feelings in my heart. This churning inside, however, was nothing more than God calling me to Himself, mixed with me trying to ignore it. I had been told time and time again that I was "all right." But I did not feel "all right," and all their assurances did not make it any better.

"What will I ever do with this troubled heart of mine? It does not seem like it will ever be content!" I cried out to the Lord, weeping in prayer as He was about disappear over the ridge in front of me.

"I simply cannot live with this. I must do something to relieve this passion of soul and spirit, or else I must remove this anxious heart from me. Somehow, I must find rest."

I did not realize that, with those few words spoken in sheer exasperation, my world was about to change in ways I could not imagine. As I stood weeping on the river's edge, it seemed as though nature itself crashed to a halt. The turbulent waters behind me were suddenly silent. The Lord stopped and turned around. Heaven itself held its breath.

Chapter Ten

"What did I say?" I looked around for an answer. The Lord began quickly walking toward me. "Did I say something wrong? Is there an enemy coming?"

The Lord said nothing as He approached me.

"Lord, what did I say?" My heart began to beat louder and louder, and its pain grew beyond what I could bear. "What did I say? What did I say, Lord!?" I shouted almost uncontrollably as the sound of my beating heart rose to a deafening thunder. I was certain it was about to explode when I began to hear the sound of another heart. It was the Lord's heart. His heart raced as mine raced. His heart grew louder as my heart grew louder. It became almost impossible to tell them apart as they beat with the same rhythm.

But the pain—the pain grew greater and greater, if that were possible. The Lord stood and simply held out His hands to me. Immediately, I knew just what to do, what I had to do, what I was desperate to do for so many years. I ran to Him with all the speed my legs could gather. I thought I would never get to Him. I fell to His feet as I reached inside to my heart.

"Ahhhh, blessed relief!" I cried to myself as the pain and the ache were suddenly gone. But there in my hands was my aching, burning, beating heart. With tears streaming down my face, I gave it to Him as reverently, as worshipfully as I knew how. Through streaming tears, I managed a few meager words. "This is Yours, my Lord. It is Yours." As I handed it to Him, fire blazed from its center. It seemed to leap for joy as I carefully placed my heart, my will, into His hands. For the first time in my life, my heart, my deepest desire, and my will were inseparable. I could not tell them apart. My heart and my will had became one, and they belonged to my Lord and to my Lord alone.

The glow from my heart's fire fell on the face of my Lord. I could not help staring at Him. He smiled with tears of joy also streaming down His face.

"Look at your heart," the Lord said to me. "Look closely at what has happened to it."

It is difficult to find human words for what I saw. Here was this living organ. Was it natural? Spiritual? This dimension or another dimension? It glowed with eternal fire so bright I could hardly resist shielding my eyes. Its colors changed moment by moment to every shade of white's ethereal brightness. Then there were streaks of lavender and scarlet; then to white again with traces of emerald; and then back to white lavender and scarlet again. Its beauty filled the early evening sky and seemed to be telling all of creation the glory and majesty of God's love.

In fact, as I was consumed by this supernatural phenomenon, I began to hear such glorious voices singing of the wonders of the Lord. The light danced in ecstatic joy to the music. I looked for angels singing but then realized that it was the light shining from my heart that was singing and dancing and worshiping, straining with every possible means to express the absolute joy and contentment of yielding to the Lord. The light sang songs in languages I had never heard and did not understand with the human mind. But my heart certainly understood and certainly yielded itself completely to these heavenly songs. These were new songs, filling the natural and spiritual atmospheres for the first time ever, for they were being sung as they were written deep in my heart.

The beating of my heart had turned to worship. It beat with joy, with contentment, and with power as the light engulfed that riverbank.

Soon angels appeared around us. It was as though the light had become a beacon into eternity hailing angels from throughout the universe. They shouted with joyful resolve as they broke through time and space, "The Lord God almighty! Full of compassion and mercy."

As far as I could see, angelic beings joined this triumphal celebration of His love and tender mercies.

A myriad of angels flew from left to right singing, "Who is like unto Thee, full of compassion to a thousand generations?" Another myriad flew from right to left, extolling the virtues of the Lord. "Who is like Thee among the gods, O Lord? Who is like Thee, majestic in holiness, awesome in praises, working wonders?" One sang as it flew from the left, "Full of grace and healing." Another sang as it flew from the right, "The Lord God showing His loving-kindness to all who call upon Him."

My gaze returned to the Lord, who was looking intently at my heart still resting in His hands. The Lord said, "Look again," nodding toward my heart. There, amid the light and song, my heart opened to its deepest, most hidden place. There, I saw a most unbelievable sight. For there were His laws—at least some of them—written clearly and gently by the finger of God.

"You have allowed Me to begin writing My ways on your heart," the Lord said to me. "Do you know what this means?"

Of course, I did not. "I do not understand, my Lord. Why is all this happening? What is going on? Why are the angels here? Why is this so wonderful, so important?"

The Lord did not answer me immediately, but instead raised His hands, moving my heart closer to His. The songs of the angels ceased as they quickly gathered around that little patch of stone and sand.

"Now salvation belongs to the Lord!" One angel shouted as he stepped forward from the crowd of angels surrounding us. "Now the enemy of your soul has been cast down, and the Lord will rule and reign forever and ever."

The closer my heart got to His, the more spectacular was the response. The lights turned into streams of living fire that lifted songs of worship and love to the Lord. Light greater than a hundred suns seemed to radiate from my heart. Creation itself seemed to be watching, waiting.

But in a moment, it was over. The Lord placed my heart into His own. All was quiet again, except for the river that now raged behind me instead of in front of me.

The Lord took my hand and knelt down in front of me to look into my eyes.

"Now I will answer your question," He said with a radiant smile. "The holiest place in all the universe is the place of divine union—the place where man gives up his will to his Lord. Of all the creatures in the universe, none were made to instinctively lay down their will for another, putting their life at risk. But you have done this most unnatural, but most spiritual thing. You have trusted the Lord your God, giving up your will for the will of your Lord's. This, My son, is a most holy response to God.

"The Most Holy Place is the place where you trust your Lord at your point of greatest risk. You must believe Him against all logic, all instinct, against everything your mind uses against you. Union becomes the experience of this trust and the outworking of your obedience to His will. It is a love response so sincere, a devotion to your Lord so innocent, that you immediately do what you hear your Father in Heaven saying, knowing His perfect love and desire toward you.

"And Abraham believed God, and it was reckoned to him as righteousness."

Section Three

Chapter Eleven

glanced over my shoulder for one last look at the river as we walked away.

It did not seem to be as foreboding as it did when I crossed. The terrible roaring of the flowing water today seemed to be more of a song of hope and deliverance. Wildflowers lined the path we were on, and the air was filled with their aroma and with the sound of birds singing from tree to tree. The warm sun on my face reminded me of the fire the angels had built for me on the other side.

Best of all, I was walking with my Lord. His arm was on my shoulder as we walked. His nearness was giving me strength and the touch of His Presence assured me of His tender love.

"It is as though I have been born again, again, Lord. It is as though I have never known You."

"You have moved into a new dimension of My Love," the Lord responded. "Your war is over. You can spend your time with Me, fulfilling your destiny, rather than in fighting your enemies."

"You mean the enemies of my soul are gone? I will never face them again?" I asked hopefully.

The Lord shook His head. "I said that your war was over. Your enemies had you convinced that the war still raged, but the war is over. If you choose to live in My Kingdom, where My enemies are defeated, you will have peace. If you choose to live in territory where the enemy still prowls, you will, well, you will live as though the war was lost. You must trust Me."

"But, Lord, sometimes You do not seem to be so near. Sometimes I am alone."

"I have prepared a place for you, so that where I am living, you also may be living."

"But I cannot see as You see. I cannot resist..."

"Take courage, and do not be afraid." Once again, the Lord mercifully interrupted my whining.

"Until now you have been content to see only what others have told you was in the Spirit. Really, you have not seen at all. That is all about to change.

"Your eyes will be opened. You will see into the Spirit. You will see things as they really are. Your ears will hear clearly. You will not be content to hear only what others think they have heard, but you will clearly hear My voice and understand as you have never understood before.

"Your life is changing more radically than you can imagine. My Kingdom is a place of peace and safety. It is a place where the lame leap like a deer, the tongue of the dumb shouts for joy, and refreshing waters break forth from the driest places of your heart. It is a place where streams gush from your innermost being. My Kingdom is a place where deserts become pools and dry land is covered with forests."

The Lord suddenly stopped. It seemed like He was looking straight through me as He said, "There is a highway in My Kingdom, a roadway. It is called the Highway of Holiness. The unclean do not travel on it. It will be for him whose heart is set on walking that way.

"Fools will not wander on it. No lion will be there, nor will any vicious beast go up on it. These will not be found there. It is a safe place for the redeemed to walk and to live. It is in My Kingdom. I have conquered the enemy.

"The ransomed of the Lord will use it to return to Zion, the place of My Presence. They will come with joyful shouting, with everlasting joy. They will find gladness and joy there. All sorrow and sighing will flee away."

"Lord," I started, a bit uncertain, "I know we will experience all this in the future, in Heaven, but I do not..."

"Have you never read, 'I AM that I AM'? I AM not the God of the past or of the future. I AM the God of the present.

"Only a confused and insecure religion pushes My promises just far enough into the future that they cannot be touched by a hungry humanity. But all of My promises are 'yes' and 'so be it.' It is not for man to build dividing walls out of their own fears and intellectual doctrines. This Kingdom of Mine is a wonderful place. You will love living here."

He turned, and again we began to walk. It was so exhilarating! I had so much to learn about His ways, so much to experience.

I took His hand and held it close to me.

"Come," He smiled, "walk with Me."

We went on silently for some distance.

"Where *are* we going?" I finally asked.

"Home," the Lord said rather matter-of-factly. "We are going home."

"Your home or my home?" I responded.

"Our home."

"Our home? I am going to live with You?"

"In My Father's house there are many dwelling places. I told you I had prepared a place for you, and so I have."

Just then we arrived at what appeared to be a camp of some sort. It seemed to be a tent with a wall around it. At least, there used to be a wall around it. The walls were so old, so tattered. It was obviously not in use, and probably abandoned for a very long time.

"Ah, here we are," the Lord said.

I must have looked as surprised as I felt.

"Here we are?" I asked as we stepped over debris from what seemed to be years of neglect. There were broken pots and mangled animal cages of every sort and description. The animal skin walls were down almost the entire perimeter of "home." A huge table had weeds growing around it and on it. Its blackened surface and strange markings down the sides did not give me a clue as to what had gone on here. A large stone washbasin lay cracked and tilted to one side.

The remains of thousands of broken and weather-battered tents dotted the land surrounding the area where we stood. Most of the tents were partially covered with sand. None of them seemed habitable.

Desert grasses and a few hardy wildflowers grew among them.

Strangely enough, there were people everywhere, dressed in the same kind of tattered designer clothing as the weatherbeaten tent material. They did not acknowledge the Lord's Presence or my own. They were slowly sifting through the scattered debris as though aimlessly looking for something, anything, of value. It seemed odd, though, that they did not really appear as if they would actually find whatever it was they were looking for.

The Lord carefully stepped over the rocks and discarded items on the ground as we continued to walk further through the tent.

"This is home?" I tried again. "How can this be home?"

"Do you trust Me?"

"I trust you, Lord."

We kept walking.

The Lord did not attempt to talk to the people around us as we walked.

"Why do the people ignore You?" I finally asked.

"They do not see Me."

"Why do they not see You?"

"They are not looking for Me."

"But, You mean they do not see You walking here among them?"

"Some people see only what they want to see.

"Others see only what they are told to see.

"Still others pretend to see," He said.

"But none see?"

"None."

"Like the blind leading the blind?"

"Something like that."

"So will You leave them here to burn in the sun and breathe dust into their lungs and have no hope and no..." The Lord interrupted me.

"What do you think?"

Immediately I could see the love He had for these folk. Immediately I understood. He is really quite a remarkable Lord, you know.

"I think," I began, "that You are working in their hearts as You have worked in my heart. I think You are wooing these folks as You have wooed me. I think You are waiting for someone to say 'yes', and the moment they do, You will go to them as You have come to me. Then You will show them the wonders of Your awesome Kingdom just as You are showing me."

The Lord turned to me and smiled. We kept walking.

The next area was as sparsely furnished as the first. There was an old broken table, a candelabra, and another piece of furniture I could not recognize. The ground was littered with unidentifiable artifacts as worthless as the tumbleweed that the wind blew through the tattered tent walls.

The people continued their aimless search in total silence. Their eyes held no hope as they fingered through the dusty rubble on the ground. They did not seem to realize that there were others around them. Each seemed consumed in his own world of heartache and hopelessness.

I looked carefully for something that seemed to have value. But I realized that I was in the same room they were in. The only difference between myself and those who crawled on the floor was the Lord. I saw the Lord, they saw only rubble.

"Hummm, so this is home," I tried to encourage myself as we moved toward the back of the tent. "Definitely a fixer-upper."

The wind continued to blow briskly through the broken walls. The sides flapped loudly, and small dusty whirlwinds blew over the ground. This was certainly not the scene to prepare me for what was just beyond the final curtain.

Chapter Twelve

The Lord went in first, opening the curtain from the center. He turned to me with a gracious smile and the invitation, "Come in, sit with Me."

As I followed Him, I suddenly realized where we were. I also realized what I had missed as we walked through the first two rooms of the tabernacle of Moses. We had just stepped into the Holy of Holies.

The Ark of the Covenant was in the center of the room with the cherubim on either side, just as the Scriptures had said. The poles that used to carry the Ark were lying on the ground parallel to the Ark, exactly where they should be lying. But this room was different than the other rooms. This room was obviously cared for. The gold overlaid on the Ark and the cherubim that were stationed on either side of it glowed a nearly blinding white from the pulsating ethereal Light that rested between the wings of the angels that guarded it. Fresh blood lay on the Mercy Seat and streamed down the front of the Ark to form small pools that completely encircled the Ark at its base.

"I do not understand, Lord. The tabernacle seems abandoned except for this room. Why are there no Levites? Where did this fresh Blood come from?"

"The Blood of the Lamb of God is eternal Blood, living Blood. It was shed one time, yet always intercedes for the world, always flows, always calls to dying humanity to 'come'."

He walked toward the Ark, toward the Mercy Seat that covered it. He stood for a moment there and then turned and sat down.

"Come, My son, sit with Me."

"Come sit with You?" I asked.

The Lord smiled, "Yes, come sit with Me."

"You want me to sit with You there on the Mercy Seat?"

"Yes, I do."

"Is that what You meant when You invited me here? You want me to sit with You? This is home?"

"This is home. Come," He said again, "sit with Me."

"Lord, how can I do that? How can it be? Maybe someday when the last of my enemies are vanquished. Maybe when I get rid of my shame…"

"I have removed your shame by the very Blood you see on this Seat," the Lord interrupted me.

I noticed the Blood was soaking into His robe as He sat.

"But, Lord, I do not belong there. I am such a screwup. I would discredit the gospel."

The Lord began to laugh out loud. I was a bit confused to see His reaction to my sincere concern.

"Lord, You know what people say when someone is caught in one sin or another. You know how people brand someone when he shows a weakness. They have no mercy. Their gossip runs wild. They relish in another's failure and broadcast it to the world. I do not want to do this to you."

Chapter Twelve

The Lord laughed again. "Lord, please do not laugh," I started.

"Then stop saying that you would discredit the gospel," He said. "The only thing that discredits the gospel is the ruthlessness of religion that cannot and will not forgive even when someone cries out in deepest repentance. Remember...

"I forgave before anyone repented.

"I forgave while humanity was in its darkest hour.

"I forgave before it ever entered into the heart of man that he had sinned.

"The greatest demonstration of My love is the ability to gather, forgive, and heal the one who has fallen."

"But what shall I do with what people say?" I asked.

"You cannot control the words of another, nor can you live your life based on an angry or jealous man's scrutiny. If it is in someone's heart to malign you, he will find something or make something up. You cannot live your life with these as your judges. There is only one Judge and Lawgiver, and He has judged you as being righteous.

"Listen, My son, you will always recognize the brokenness of another by the mercy he shows to one who is caught in sin."

"Lord, You mean, 'by the one who falls into sin'."

"No, I mean 'by the one who is caught in sin'. For all have sinned and fall short of My Glory. All sin and fall short of the Mercy Seat. That is what My Blood is for. It takes you where you cannot take yourself. Those who gossip and relish in another's misfortune do not see themselves in the pitiful condition they are in without the Lord."

I was stunned at His mercy. He continued.

"It is time that you stop responding to man and his shallow understanding of My grace and begin to believe Me.

"Now, come, sit with Me."

Again I argued. I guess I had more religion inside of me than I realized. But thank God for His patience.

"Lord, I have all these enemies. It is embarrassing to sit with You on the Mercy Seat with all these guys still inside. What would You think of me?"

The Lord looked at me as though He was about to tell me something He had wanted to say for a very long time. He was.

"You talk as though I do not already know what is deep inside of you, like you have successfully hidden some of the worst things from Me. Do you think that is possible?"

Again, shocked that I did not get what seemed to be so simple, I had nothing to say.

Can the Lord look exasperated? If so, He seemed to be so with me.

"My love for you is so simple. You must run to Me and not away from Me.

"The only hope you have of ultimate deliverance from these enemies of yours is to come and sit at My right hand, until I make your enemies a footstool for your feet. For I will stretch forth My strong scepter from Zion, the place of My manifest Presence, saying, 'Rule in the midst of your enemies.'"

"But, Lord, wasn't our Father talking about You?"

"Of course He was. He was talking about Me and everyone who is in Me. My Blood covers you until My power delivers you. Come and sit at My right hand."

Chapter Twelve

There was nothing more to say. He who had delivered me from the Egypt of my sinful slavery, who had brought me safely through the wilderness and across the river of my humanity, was now calling me to do the unthinkable, the unimaginable. He wanted me to do what defied logic and everything I had been taught. But it was He who called me.

I believed Him. Without saying a word I began to move. My eyes fixed on His eyes. My hope fixed on His word to me.

I walked slowly to the Mercy Seat and sat beside my Lord. I looked straight into His face, and I lived.

Chapter Thirteen

No sooner had I taken my seat beside the Lord when Pride appeared behind me, whispering quietly into my ear.

"Just think of it! Here you are, sitting on the Mercy Seat with Jesus Himself. I bet there are not too many people who can say that!"

The Lord turned His head toward me ever so slightly.

"Lord!" I moved a little closer to Him. "Pride is here. What am I going to say to him?"

"You are going to say nothing to him," was the Lord's first reply. He held me closer. "Center your thoughts on whatever is pure, whatever is holy, whatever is a good report."

"Yes, Lord. Thank You. You are right. You are so powerful, Your love so complete. You are far stronger than anything that attacks me."

And with that, Pride was gone.

It was great sitting with the Lord. The fellowship was so sweet. One day I realized how long it had been since I was tempted and how long it had been since I really fell into sin.

"I do not think I have sinned since I have come to sit with You, Lord. Pretty cool, huh? I am really doing good. I must be stronger than I thought."

How foolish I was not see Pride's deceptive attack. I had not even noticed his approach.

Before I realized what had happened, Pride invited Bitterness and his traveling partner Revenge to join the attack. They brazenly appeared in front of me, poisoning me with thoughts that I had always loved to dwell on. I fell for it immediately. There I was, sitting with my Lord on the Mercy Seat while feeding my soul with bitterness and plotting revenge upon those I was sure I had forgiven.

I grew more angry as Bitterness replayed events long forgotten. I should have known Bitterness was near. He was always able to remind me of the bitter details of things I could never remember on my own!

The more I remembered, the more anger became rooted in my mind. The more angry I became, the more I plotted; the more I plotted, the more Revenge and Bitterness were strengthened until they called in Rage to take charge. I seriously feared Rage. Rage was a powerful enemy. I was almost defenseless against him. If he were to step in, I would be finished.

Suddenly, I felt the Lord squeezing my hand. I did not even look at Him. I knew. I had given in to these enemies and had been sidetracked from sweet fellowship with my Lord.

"Lord, I have sinned! I messed up! I know it. But Lord, damn these people for what they did to me! If it was not for them, this would not have happened to me today. These enemies could not have gotten to me! These people always keep me from you. They always make me sin!"

Chapter Thirteen

Oh, how our discernment is tainted when we allow Pride into our lives!

The Lord turned to me with compassion and forgiveness pouring out of His eyes and directly into mine. At that moment, I was free from the attack. Pride and his platoon of mockers fled for the hills, ranting and jeering all the way.

"My God, why did that happen? I thought I was stronger than that!" I was so exasperated with myself. "Lord, I sinned! I listened to Pride! Why do I believe that trash? Now what am I going to do?"

"You know what to do," the Lord spoke to me while putting His arm around me.

"No, I do not know! I failed. I blew it." Grabbing His hand and removing it from my shoulder, I shouted through my angry tears, "How can You stand to even look at me!? I am just a screwup—just a screwup!"

I jumped off the Mercy Seat and began running from His Presence.

"Where are you going, My son? There is nothing out there. There is nowhere to go!"

But I ignored Him as I ran in my shame. "You are such a hopeless wreck," I scolded myself. "You had the best thing going, and you messed up!"

I was so embarrassed, humiliated, and angry at myself. What was I going to do? Where would I go? What would I do to win my Lord's favor again? How could I show Him how much I still loved Him?

I stopped as I ran through the remnants of the Tabernacle. I saw all these people still working on the floor, groveling through the rubble for something to give them hope. I looked at them with pity and pride. How could they be so blind? How could they be so close and yet so far from Him?

But now, I was just like them. I, too, was so close, yet so far.

There must be something, some way of proving my love to Him.

I had an idea.

"I know! Maybe if I clean this room for the Lord, He will be happy with me again. These folks are just rummaging through this stuff looking for something worthwhile. There is nothing here to find. But I will clean the room for my Lord. I will restore its glory! I will restore the priesthood!"

Quickly I began working. I fixed the table that would hold the Bread of His Presence. Then I went to the candlesticks that I had stupidly called a candelabra. I worked for hours, maybe days, trying to polish it again. But the work made me feel good.

"Surely He sees me now. Surely He sees my efforts to restore the glory of the Holy Place." I often looked over my shoulder to see if He was watching. The more I polished, the harder I worked, and the more the sweat poured over my brow, the more certain I was that He saw and was pleased. All the while, I was desperately waiting for the sense of His Presence to return. But it never came. It was as though He was ignoring my efforts.

He was.

"Come back, My son!" the Lord called to me again and again. "Your only hope is with Me. Your only hope is to come back. There is no forgiveness in the Holy Place, and none in the Outer Court. There is no blood there that has the power to remove the guilt of sin."

Chapter Thirteen

"How can I go back after what did? I need some time. God needs some time. I have to prove to Him I am serious about following Him."

So I polished and I worked and I polished even more. But His Presence did not return.

I reluctantly began to realize that the Lord was right. I tossed the candlesticks to the ground in despair and humiliation.

"He's right," I admitted to myself. "My work on the candlesticks will not please Him."

I peered through the Outer Court and then finally to the open land beyond. There was no priesthood there, no blood, no way to find forgiveness. It was hopeless. I slumped to the ground in tears of hopeless rejection. I was finished. There was no hope for me. I had surely forfeited my future, my Lord, and my hope with my stupid sin.

But through my sobs, I could faintly hear the songs my heart sang to the Lord when He gathered me to Himself after I crossed the river. Songs of love, songs of devotion and desire for Him, no matter what the cost. I slowly turned my face back to the Lord. To my surprise and relief, He was standing only inches from me.

My heart instantly re-discovered the joyful rhythm of beating with His heart. We immediately returned to wonderful, intimate fellowship together, singing of His everlasting kindness and forgiveness.

I began learning some very difficult lessons.

I was punishing myself for my failure.

He had already forgiven me.

I had sentenced myself to my own purgatory.

He was looking at me with joyful anticipation.

I looked at myself with disdain and disgust.

He held His arms open to me as the song in our hearts sang of His majesty in tender harmony.

What could I do? I fell on Him, throwing my arms around Him with sobs of grateful repentance.

"Oh Lord, You know that in my heart, I joyfully agree with Your laws, but this war waging against my mind makes me a prisoner of the sin I hate…it is too much."

The Lord said nothing, He only held me with the tenderness I had become so used to feeling.

But it did not stop the frustration I had with myself. "Wretched man that I am!" I cried out. "Who will set me free from this weakness, from this death trap of a body?"

I lifted my head to my Lord. I knew who would deliver me.

"Oh Lord, on the one hand I am serving You with my mind, my heart, my desire. But my fleshly self, my will, is still so weak. But I refuse to go back. I refuse to think that the wilderness or even Egypt is an option. But what do I do? How can I go on with this struggle?

"I mean, no one knows what I go through. No one knows what is still screaming for attention deep inside. I am such a hypocrite! Can I avoid condemnation for the way I act?"

The Lord spoke with the same soft assurance that always draws me back to reality.

"There is no condemnation for those who are in Me." His words were confident and sure.

"Come sit with Me, so that I can fight your battles and destroy the enemies of your soul. You cannot win the war. I have already won the war.

"Why do you choose to live in the land still claimed by your enemies? Come live with Me, live in Me, in territory that is Mine. I will conquer your enemies and make your land My land.

"Hypocrisy is not a matter of action but of heart. Your genuinely painful struggle and hatred of these things proves your heart is toward the Lord. Your heart is dedicated to doing what is right."

"Then why do I feel such guilt, such condemnation?" I asked.

"The flesh and religion are strange bedfellows," the Lord began, "for while seeming to be working against one another, they actually confirm one another's rebellion against the love of God. Religion can tell you that what you are doing is fine, but the guilt and shame remain. Only My Blood can truly wash away the guilt and shame of your transgression.

"The flesh, on the other hand, will always support the legalism and control of religion, knowing that that will ensure the absence of My Presence. True conviction and repentance are only accomplished by Me.

"When I say you are forgiven, My words penetrate the deepest recesses of who you are, freeing you from the harassing guilt of your sin and the condemning memory that religion wants you to carry.

"Genuine forgiveness renews your resolve and brings deliverance to your life. There is no amount of church attendance, Bible memory, or correct dress that can bring that about. My Presence alone brings true freedom from the residue of sin."

I sat there holding Him as He spoke. I could not tell whether He was actually speaking to me or if we were communicating spirit to Spirit. But, I did not really care. He was with me. He forgave me. He was healing me.

"Let's go home," the Lord said gently. "Let's go home."

Chapter Fourteen

In the blink of an eye, we were back on the Mercy Seat. We sat quietly while virtue flowed from His Spirit into the depths of my soul.

It was all such a strange experience. I was not the same person anymore. I really did want Him, and my failure into sin did not change that. I began to see that I did not run from Him because I wanted to go back to Egypt after I had sinned; instead, I ran because I had failed Him. I still wanted Him more than anything else in the world. The thought of hurting Him, of letting Him down, was more than I could bear.

Something incredible had changed. Sin no longer was my master. I did not crave Egypt as I once had. I did not need Egypt. I coveted my Lord. Sin was not an escape to merely gratify an old fleshly desire. It was an enemy, something that I hated, something that kept me from the One whom my soul doth love. Yes, sin was ever threatening, but I was no longer its slave. I had a new allegiance, a new hope, a new destination.

I had to remember that He loved me more than I could ever love Him. His love for me was not dependent upon my correct response, a right attitude, or a right action. He loved me, well, because He chose to love me.

He is not like us.

He forgives and forgets.

We remember and punish.

He understands our humanity.

We try to ignore it.

His love lasts forever.

Our love lasts as long as it is convenient.

He covers another's failure.

We broadcast them to the world.

He is patient with our limitations.

We are patient only with our own.

No, our Lord is not much like us. He draws us continually to Himself, in spite of our humanity.

Learning to stay on the Mercy Seat and to yield to His love and forgiveness is only one step away from yielding to His will and the dreams He has dreamed for our lives. There, on the seat of ultimate mercy, He fights our battles, frees us from our tormentors, and shields us from the accuser of the brethren so we can give ourselves openly, freely, fearlessly to Him, the Lover of our souls.

Chapter Fifteen

"*L*ord, I am sorry for asking; it is probably none of my business, but I just do not understand the neglected condition of the Tabernacle. Why is it that this room is so awesome, but the rest of the temple is so completely useless?"

"How did you feel as you ran away from Me through the ruins?" my Lord asked softly.

"I felt terrible. It was frightening, hopeless, even confusing. I would not admit it, but I knew as soon as I left this Seat that I would have to return to get free from the guilt and shame."

"That is right, and so you should have. The ruins of the Outer Court and the Holy Place are a continuous reminder of the utter barrenness of human effort and monotonous religious activity."

"There I was, trying to rebuild the ruins of human effort, and all the while You were calling me to come to You freely, openly, completely." I shook my head and shuddered. "Lord, I couldn't imagine myself on that floor for the rest of my life, just digging through the rubble, polishing candlesticks that did not even matter, looking for some kind of meaning to my life. It brought back such painful memories of searching for You but never finding You!"

The Lord gave me a reassuring hug, so I went on, "I felt bad for the people around me. I tried to talk to them, but they acted like I had a disease. I was not even preaching to them, although I wanted to. I just tried to begin any kind of a conversation. It is so lonely out there! It seemed everyone was afraid to talk to each other. You know, really talk."

I turned to the Lord, realizing I was finally able to express what my heart had been burning to say. "But, Lord, to be honest, I wasn't lonely for people. I was lonely for You!"

The Lord squeezed my shoulders again, and I continued, "Even while I sat out there polishing the candlesticks, I realized that just the memory of Your Presence, the memory of sitting with You, had ruined me for religion. No matter what happened, I could never live there again."

I looked away from His gaze briefly, paused for a moment, and then looked back into His eyes. "I secretly hoped You would come and rescue me," I confessed.

The Lord chuckled. "Yes, I know. That is why I came for you. You finally, once again, had had enough of religion."

"But how long will those people be satisfied with less than Your Presence?"

"You can answer that one," the Lord replied.

He was right. I knew the answer. I had to come to the end of myself, my pride, my reputation, my career, my ministry, and even my family. In fact, I had to resist everything and everyone who tried to tell me that I was crazy, that God could never be that real.

Chapter Fifteen

For me, the turning point in my search came in a dream. In this dream, I appeared before the Lord after I had died. He asked me why I had not listened to His persistent beckoning. Knowing I was I in trouble, I gave Him every reason I could think of for not responding to Him. I even tried to give Him a Bible study on how obeying leadership was right, holy, and scriptural, even when I knew the Lord had spoken something different to my heart than leadership was willing to believe.

I was so glad to wake up from that dream. It was then that I determined I would "romance" Him.

But I still did not understand how the Tabernacle got into such disrepair.

"Lord," I began. He interrupted before I could ask the question.

"Remember our walk among the children of Israel in the wilderness? I think it is time for a visit to another place, in another time."

As usual we were there before I could respond.

Chapter Sixteen

"Wow! Now this is the Tabernacle! This is the real thing!" I said with great delight. "So this is what it looks like in full operation! Marvelous, indeed!"

The Tabernacle, along with the surrounding camp, bustled with activity in the early morning sunlight. Manna was gathered quickly and put into leather pouches while children laughed as they made a game of catching the manna flakes on their tongues as it fell like snow to the ground.

Fathers tended fires and carried water to the family tent.

"Yes," the Lord began, "this is what it looks like with the purposes of God resting on it, in the first days after the children of Israel left Egypt.

"The other temple we walked through is the real Tabernacle too, as real as this one. This one is just in another time, another dimension.

"Come, walk with Me. I have a lot to show you today."

Naturally, He smiled as He walked among His people. He laid His hand on some, whispered softly and lovingly into the ears of others, and blessed everyone. I was enjoying how He loved them, cared for them. You could see it in His eyes, in the gentleness with which He touched them and prayed for them. They were clearly His own special treasure.

We soon arrived at the entrance to the Tabernacle. I stood back from all the activity, not knowing what was about to happen.

In the misty dampness of the early morning, the priests were already busy with the sacrifices of the day. They were already covered in sweat with the work of the altar and the heat of the burning fire. The altar dripped with blood and had already soaked the ground beneath it.

I had no idea how bloody and dirty this job was. The robes of the priests were drenched with both the splattered blood from the sacrificed animals and the sweat that rolled down their faces. Dust, feathers, and animal hair clung to the blood and sweat on their garments.

What a mess! I thought to myself.

"It is early in the day," the Lord answered my thought. "It will be worse as the day goes on."

I never dreamed they worked this hard or that it was such a…a rough job. I watched them slaughter animals one after another and prepare them for burning by removing their entrails and…well, I think you get the picture. It was rough.

I wondered that men would work so hard knowing that their efforts would never take away the guilt or stain of sin. Day after day, year after year, they never seemed to get it.

"It is not so different in your time," the Lord answered my thoughts again.

"But, Lord, their efforts are hopeless. The best animals, the purest blood, the purest heart—even all together they could not accomplish the freedom from guilt they wanted."

"Your religion is no different."

"It's not my religion anymore," I replied with conviction and resolve. "I have repented of lifeless form and ritual."

The Lord smiled at me without a word and went on.

"Religion will never satisfy. It will never fill the hunger deep within the human heart. It can never bring true freedom to the heart that is riddled by guilt and shame.

"It will never bring you to God's glory. Just as the blood of bulls and goats cannot grant forgiveness of sins, neither can the dead works of hopeless and monotonous religious activity. It only produces sweat, and sweat is the wrong blood.

"Sweat, no matter how well intentioned, cannot take away sins.

"But today, everything changes. This is a very special day in the life of Israel," the Lord said to me. "The Lamb of God will be sacrificed. He will carry the cup of His own Blood to the Mercy Seat.

"Stand back a little, My son. You are about to see what occurred in eternity the day the Son of man was sacrificed."

"Yes, Lord." Of course. I had so many questions, but even I know when to keep quiet and just watch.

The Lord Jesus, the Lamb of God, approached the priests at the altar of sacrifice. He came out of the shadows as One whom they did not recognize. The priests looked at Him a bit puzzled, but they never stopped to talk. They were too busy doing the work of the Lord. They were too busy making the sacrifices and gathering the blood that would never take away sin or the guilty conscience that went with it.

The Lord walked closer to them, close enough so that He was in their way. His Presence was becoming a nuisance. It was difficult for them to work. Finally one of the priests bumped into the Lord. I did not think it was an accident, but, hey, I was not going to interfere.

"Excuse me!" the priest spoke gruffly to the Lord.

"No, no," the Lord replied, "excuse *Me*." But the Lord did not move from His place. He actually inched in a little closer. He stood there patiently watching them work. It did not seem to bother Him that the splattering blood of the sacrifices was now falling on His garments. The way He concentrated on the priests made me wonder whether or not He even knew.

It did not take long for another priest to find cause to push the Lord to one side.

"Excuse me! Excuse me!" came the impatient voice of the priest. "Exactly what are you doing here? You are not a priest. You are a common sinner, the laity. You do not belong here."

At that moment, the Lord was shoved again by yet another priest. "Excuse me!" came the now programmed response from the priests. "We have work to do here. We are doing the work of the Lord. Do not interfere with our God-ordained program. We know what we are doing."

The Lord walked to the edge of the altar and, with the compassionate voice of the Son of God, He said, "No, you must excuse *Me*."

It was so strange. They actually made way for Him as He approached. A thousand questions must have filled their minds as they stared at Him walking to the altar. They were beginning to realize that He intended to somehow perform the duties of a priest. Yet, no one dared to stop Him. He silently looked deep into their eyes. Their defiance was rigid. "He is not a priest!" one finally shouted indignantly. "He cannot touch the holy things!"

"I AM the holy thing!" was His triumphant reply.

The priests dropped everything they were doing and stared in stunned silence. The Lord leaned His body over the entire width of the altar. Stretching His arms as far as He could, He swept the remains of a lamb just sacrificed from the altar and let it fall rather sacrilegiously to the floor. He cleared the altar of every trace of the animal.

"I am the Lamb of God," He said softly. "I have come to take away the sin of the world."

The priests mumbled to themselves and to each other, being much too shocked to raise another objection to the Lord Himself.

Then He pointed to one of the priests with finality and confidence. "You are dismissed," He said quietly. Moving His finger to yet another priest, He repeated His brazen command, "You are dismissed." Then to another and another and still another. "You are all dismissed!"

Pointing to the only remaining priest, He said, "You have but one final sacrifice to make, the sacrifice for which your priesthood exists, and then you are dismissed. You are all dismissed."

Well, no one questioned what He had just done. But they wondered to themselves, "What does He mean? Dismissed? One final sacrifice?"

He knew their thoughts but did not bother to answer them. He looked down at the altar He had just cleared. He laid His hands on the cold stone and leaned His body against it for just a moment. Then He turned His eyes to His Father. He took a deep breath as He smiled heavenward. "Nevertheless," He prayed softly, "not My will, but Your will be done."

Before anyone had time to wonder what that meant, He lifted Himself on to Aaron's altar. Reaching for the knife lying at His feet, He looked once again at a disbelieving priesthood. "With this final sacrifice, your priesthood is dismissed." Then He handed the knife to the nearest priest.

The priests were livid. "How dare You profane the work of God! This is blasphemy! How dare You mock the sacred altar! There is a penalty for mocking the sacred altar, You know!"

The Lord lifted His head long enough to look deep into their eyes, as though pouring all His love into them and offering them one last opportunity for repentance.

"I know the penalty for mocking the sacred altar." He spoke with such compassion to those who were about to slay Him. "I know the penalty." Then He lowered His head once again.

The Lord lay there, fully knowing what He was doing and what was about to happen. He spoke once more to the priests. "Do your religious duty." The priests rushed upon Him and killed Him there where He lay, of course, as was required by the Law.

The priests walked away from His body with self-righteous confidence, congratulating themselves for their courage and religious zeal to protect the work of God. All the while, they missed the Son of God who had stood in their presence, ultimately killing Him in their sanctimonious blindness and religious piety.

As the priests walked away from the altar, they all vanished. They had been dismissed.

I was shocked as I witnessed this incredible event. I was far more struck, however, by the sight of the Blood of Jesus falling to the ground. I could not believe it.

"There is no one to catch the Blood!" I shouted out loud. Of course, no one could hear me, but I was too stunned to remember that.

"This is pretty important Blood to let it just fall to the ground, don't you think?" I called out loud once again. But there was no one to hear. There were no priests. The Lord had dismissed them. They did their religious duty, and then they were gone. All of them.

So what will happen now? I wondered. *How will the cup of His Blood get into the Holy of Holies?*

The cup of the Lord's Blood had to be taken into the Most Holy Place, but He had just dismissed the priesthood who should catch the Blood and deliver it to the Levites, who would present the Blood within the veil. I watched His Blood continue to drip, now forming a small pool on the ground just beneath the altar.

As I pondered these things, I suddenly remembered His resurrection. He was not just the Lamb of God; He was also the first of the order of Melchizedek! He would have to be raised from the dead in order to deliver the cup of the Blood of the sacrificed

Lamb to the Father, who dwells within the veil of the Most Holy Place.

The Lamb of God would have to become the priest of the Presence. The same Jesus who gave His life must now be raised from the dead in order to finish the work given to Him by His Father.

My eyes were fixed on Him. I was about to see Him return to life. Oh, how many times had I read about it, sung about it, talked about it. Now, I would see it happen.

Something did happen as I watched, but it was not what I expected. As I waited for the power of God to descend upon Him, smoke began to roll from under the Lord's body and around the altar. Flames quickly followed, engulfing His entire body. Far from the controlled sacrificial fires of the priests, this flame raged completely unrestrained, radiating heat and sparks in every direction. Blackened billows of smoke, rolling angrily from the flames, were captured by the wind and sent churning into the brightness of the morning sun.

I could no longer see His body or the altar He lay on. The fire raged, growing into a hideous frenzy as though determined to eliminate every remaining element of the Lord's body.

"Now we have Him!" the flames mocked as they danced and swirled around the altar upon which He lay. "Now there is no escape." They laughed. "What kind of love is that? He just let His Son die. He just gave Him to us!"

The heavens were silent in bewildered disbelief. Angels stood as though frozen as they watched the spectacle. Demons rushed from throughout the universe to join in the mockery of the Son of God. They reveled in their morbid celebration at the presumed victory in the murder of the Christ of God.

The rage of the enemy's best effort, however, would not be able to even touch the Lord. All the forces of hell would not affect Him in any time or in any dimension. Jesus had conquered death's most resolute yet pathetic attempts to eliminate His Destiny from the earth.

The Lord had defeated satan in eternity and in earth, totally and forever eliminating the possibility of another challenge to the Lord's mission on planet Earth. The enemy was once and for all finished. He had no recourse. Having engaged the Lord on every front, satan's loss was complete and unrecoverable. This vanquished foe had given his best challenge. The result was the humiliating and total destruction of the enemy's claim on God's most favored creation, humanity, through whom the Lord had predestined to show His love to a dying planet. This humanity was chosen to be the dwelling place of the Most High God, who declared to Heaven and to earth, "This is My resting place, forever! Here I will dwell forever. I have desired her!"

Still the firestorm continued to rage, as did the hopeless mockery of an obliterated army, obviously with no sense that its power was infinitely insufficient and its mission a dismal failure.

Then, as though coming in from a summer stroll with His Father, the Lord simply walked away from the altar without even a smoking strand of hair on His head. His face was radiant and His walk triumphant. He had completed salvation and made the way for humanity to complete the plan of the Father for the ages to come.

"I love reliving that," the Lord said to me with a smile. "It is always such a rush!"

"Lord!" I shouted. I am afraid I looked rather shocked at seeing Him emerge from flames. The Lord just laughed approvingly at my surprise.

"So that is how it happened! You are so awesome! That was just brilliant!" I fell to the ground in reverent and fearful worship of the One who had accomplished such a thing for me.

He smiled as He spoke to me. Holding the cup of His own Blood, He glanced down at the cup and then back to me.

"You did not need to be so concerned about My Blood. I had it covered."

He helped me to my feet, then turned and walked slowly into the Holy Place.

"Lord!" I called to Him. "Are we going on? I need some time here. Do You realize what just happened?"

I turned around to look at the still-smoldering altar as liquid rock dripped slowly from the top of the stone where Jesus had laid.

Wow, they gave it their best shot, I thought to myself as I stared.

"They gave it their only shot, My son," the Lord assured me as He approached the Table of Showbread.

Beginning to understand His power just a little bit more clearly, I decided to walk a little slower behind Him, following at a safer distance.

He immediately approached the priests who tended the table.

The priests worked diligently with the showbread, preparing it for proper placement on the table. They were way too busy with their responsibilities to notice the Presence of the Lord as they worked.

"Excuse *Me*," the Lord began.

"Excuse who?" came the rather gruff reply. They were obviously not used to being disturbed as they did the work of the Lord.

"Excuse Me," the Lord said, leaning forward slightly with a patient smile on His face.

"What are You doing here?" came the predictable response from the priest. "On second thought," the priest stopped to look at the Lord, "I really do not care what You are doing here. You are in the way, and You should not be here. We are tending to the Bread of the Presence of the Lord. You are slowing us down, confusing our routine. We know what to do. We have been doing it for years."

Suddenly they realized that they did not recognize Him as a priest at all. "We know what God wants. You are not even a priest. You have no training, no education; what do You know? Please, could You step back?"

It would have been comical if it had not reminded me of myself.

I am so busy with the work of the Lord that I forget the Lord of the work.

I forget the sense of His Presence and the sound of His voice.

I forget why I am doing what I am doing.

I never stop to ask if I am still doing what He so definitely called me to do so many years ago.

These guys were just doing what they always did with no thought that they were serving a living God who still speaks and still controls the destiny of His own Church.

I, too, had become so numb that I could not discern His nearness or understand His leading. So, I just did what came naturally. I denied reality and developed a routine that looked spiritual enough. It was good enough to convince everyone around me that I was the man of faith and power: praying, studying, singing, attending every meeting. You know, I was being spiritual. I knew how to just keep quiet and make the Bread of the Presence, or whatever bread I was making, sermon after sermon, study after study, week after week, year after year, conscientiously and reliably, dutifully if not boringly. It got to the point where I could barely stay awake for my own services and the sermons that I was preaching!

No, I could not laugh at these men, but I did feel very sorry for them. Like me, they had the very Presence of the Lord among them and could not recognize Him.

"We are making the Bread of Life," one priest said, barely looking up from his work.

"I AM the Bread of Life. I AM the Bread that comes down from Heaven."

Pointing to the priests as they did their work, the Lord declared, "You are dismissed." Before the priests had time to look up from their work, they were gone. They just disappeared as the others had.

Once again I was shocked. These priests were gone. The loaves sat there only partially prepared. The utensils lay where they dropped. The dust of the flour drifted aimlessly from the table. I refrained from asking who would finish the work there.

I understood that their work, and the bread they prepared, were no longer needed. The priesthood was replaced by Him who is the True and Living Bread of Life.

Then the Lord moved to the candlesticks, where other priests worked to keep the oil flowing and the flames burning. One priest was polishing the stand.

I know that that is a thankless job, I thought to myself. Then I realized that another conversation was about to begin. I listened as the Lord approached them.

"Excuse Me," the Lord began. "What are you doing?" He asked delightfully with the same smile.

"Who wants to know?"

"Well," the Lord began, "it would certainly go much easier if you were to ask Me to..."

"Ask You? Ask You? And just who are You and why are You in here anyway?" The priests turned to Him and took turns protecting and justifying their ministry. "This work is for the priesthood, not the common people, not for the laity," one boasted. "You need a special calling to do this work," another chimed in, as yet another priest nodded, "God does not call everyone, You know."

The Lord, full of kindness and everlasting patience (ask me how I know), countered with a smile, as usual ignoring their religious ranting. "What is your job here?"

The priests gasped. "Can't you see? We must make sure the light never goes out. We feed the candles with oil, trim the wicks, and clean the stems."

One priest proudly announced, "You might say that this is the light of the world."

Oh my, I thought to myself, *that was the wrong thing to say.*

If there was one thing I have learned, it is that I am nothing without Him and that I can do nothing without Him. He does not need me to do anything. He uses me because He chooses to show Himself to the world through Me. He chooses to shine through me.

He is the light; I am the lamp He chooses to shine through.

He feeds me with His oil.

He trims my wick when my flame gives off black smoke.

He is the One who ensures that the light will always be there.

Because *He* is, of course, the Light of the world.

"Yes," I nodded to myself, "I would say those boys are in trouble."

The Lord turned to me. He knew my thoughts.

"You are learning your lessons well, My son." Without waiting for a response, Jesus stepped back from the candles and declared,

"No, I AM the Light of the world. The sweat of human effort can never bring about my Father's glory.

"You are dismissed."

Just like the others, before any of them could protest, they were gone.

Chapter Sixteen

Only one priest remained in the Holy Place. He was tending the Altar of Incense. It was obvious that he was a bit nervous. He had watched as the Lord walked through the temple. He saw the Lord visiting and dismissing the priests whose efforts would forever now be part of the finished work of the Lord Jesus.

The Lord walked to him, smiling.

"Where have all the others gone?" the last priest asked with a nervous smile. "What have You done to them?"

"I haven't done anything to them. They have been retrenched," the Lord said with a sparkle in His eye, "assuming they can accept the new order of things. Their duties here are completed, as are yours."

"Oh, but You do not understand," this last priest began. "I tend the Altar of Incense," he continued reassuringly. "I tend to the prayers of the saints. The smoke of their needs flow up to the nostrils of the Lord. This smoke is a sweet incense to Him and to His nose."

The Lord stole a glance at me as He rubbed His nose a bit with a smile. "Is that so?"

"Oh yes, indeed." The priest went on, continuing to explain his duties to the One to whom he prophetically pointed but did not recognize. "I stand between the people and the Lord, making sure their prayers get to God."

"I AM He that ever liveth to make intercession on behalf of the saints," declared the Lord. "I alone stand between the people and their God. I alone make sure their prayers get to God. You, My friend, with all the priests of the Outer Court and the Holy Place, are dismissed. For I have gathered My people to Myself.

"They are royalty.

"They are My own special treasure.

"They are holy unto Me.

"I shall love them face to face, heart to heart, love to love.

"No longer shall a man represent Me to what is Mine or represent what is Mine to Me."

The Lord turned from the priest and spoke with finality. "You are dismissed. You have fulfilled your destiny.

"Now it is time for Me to fulfill Mine."

Chapter Seventeen

Immediately, we were alone. All was quiet. The priests who had prophetically pointed to the Christ of God had become obsolete in a moment of time. After thousands of years, the work of Aaron and Levi was finally done. Their mission was complete. Their priesthood was now fulfilled. They were dismissed, to be replaced by the reality of the One whom they had foretold time after time as they performed their duties in the temple.

No longer was there a need for the continuous sacrifices of the Outer Court, which sacrifices, I might add, did not take away the consciousness of sin or the clinging guilt that haunted them. No longer would the priests carefully collect the blood of the sacrifices that carried the form of the heavens but brought no power, no peace, and no deliverance. This blood of animal sacrifices would never be able to take away the guilt of sin in spite of their exacting rules and precise attention to detail in every aspect of their priesthood.

No longer would the brazen altar burn with the stench of sacrificial flesh. That smoke only reminded them of the futility of their offering as they awaited One whose sacrifice would truly bring the wholeness of divine favor they so desperately desired.

But now, their Deliverer, their Savior, their Lord, had finally come. In His coming, He had fulfilled everything that this priesthood had pointed to.

The Lamb of God had come, accomplishing far more than anyone had realized. He had come to take away the sin of the entire world. Now mankind would be free from the penalty of their sins and the guilt that most certainly followed. Now the true Blood had been shed and the miracle of redemption accomplished.

Now mankind would be free from the accusations that forever paralyzed them, preventing them from living where God had intended them to live and from experiencing what God had intended them to experience. Now man would accomplish his destiny and forever be free from the taunting rage of unregenerated flesh along with the relentless, overpowering control sin had in their lives. They were now servants of the One who bought them instead of slaves of the one who had stolen their future somewhere out of time.

The Levites would no longer point to the coming Savior and the redeeming virtues that were contained in Him…

The Bread of the Presence had become the Bread of Life.

The light of the candlesticks had become the Light of the world.

The table of incense had become the intercession of the Son of God.

He had come; the truth was there for all to see. The shadows had become the Son. The types had been fulfilled. Their work was now consumed by the One whom they had represented.

Chapter Seventeen

With the work of Aaron and Levi complete and their priesthood dismissed, He would now inaugurate the priesthood that had waited for the precise moment to break through time and space to fulfill its role in the plan of the ages. For this Christ, having become the Lamb of God, had risen from the dead in order to become the first priest in the order of a new and eternal priesthood. Melchizedek was about to perform His duties within the veil.

Jesus had lived from eternity past with His Father. There is no understanding of exactly how long that really was. Of course, we live in time. He lives out of time and in eternity. But we know that They had enjoyed sweet fellowship together as Father and Son. Naturally, you would think that His appearing within the veil would be a wonderful homecoming.

But this would be different. The Son would have to trust the promise of His Father. For He had carried upon Himself the sins of all mankind from every time. As the Lamb of God, He had taken upon Himself everything that His Father hated. The Son carried every rebellion, everything wicked, everything vile, everything that had caused satan to fall in a timeless past, everything that kept man from his Creator. He carried every sickness, every sorrow, every pain. Every memory that caused mankind to fall short of His glory was carried on the back of the Son of God. The Son allowed Himself to be tainted, darkened, and condemned by every evil that the mind of man and satan could contrive together throughout all time. He actually became everything sinful in order to deliver it all to hell itself, leaving it there for all time.

As I watched the Lord walk toward the torn veil with the cup of His own Blood, there was every confidence, every anticipation of a joyous, rollicking reunion. He turned to me.

"Come closer, watch what will happen."

He turned away toward the curtain, holding the cup of His own Blood in His right hand. He slowly pulled the torn veil with His left hand and walked in. The moment the curtain opened, the glorious, blinding lights of His Presence exploded from the Most Holy Place. I instinctively covered my face with my arms.

"Wow!" was the most descriptive I could get in my surprise. The Light swirled round and round, filling every crevice of the Holy Place, and then streamed through to the Outer Court and beyond.

The Light seems to have a mind of its own. It seems to be alive, I thought to myself. It raced to the horizon and expanded without losing even a bit of its brilliance. As much as I wanted to follow this unfolding drama, I turned my attention to inside the veil. This was an event I did not want to miss.

I opened the veil, ever so slightly to look in. I again shielded my eyes from the intensity of the glory within. I slowly uncovered them, hoping they would get used to the brilliance of the light. But I could not manage much more than just pale outlines in the blinding glow of His Manifest Presence.

I saw enough to be transfixed by what was happening. The Son walked slowly, reverently, confidently. He, Himself, glowed with a translucent radiance of another dimension. He was existing in two places at one time. He was in the Presence of the Father, but He was enough on this side for me to follow Him.

Chapter Seventeen

The closer He walked, the brighter the pulsating light of His Manifest Presence responded. The cherubim on either side of the Presence fidgeted slightly in anticipation of the approach of the Son. He walked within inches of the Presence. I was no longer in the Temple laid with types and shadows of what is in Heaven. I was *there*. The real cherubim glowed with exponential brilliance over the golden statues of the temple. The Mercy Seat, overlaid with gold, was the throne of the Ancient of Days, whose nature and character is mercy. And there He sat, covered with unapproachable light—light so powerful, so penetrating, so all-seeing, that mere unprotected flesh cannot survive in His Presence.

"Father," I heard Him speak softly, lovingly.

"Here it is."

He looked down at the earthenware bottle in His hand. His wounds were freshly visible as He extended His arm toward His Father.

"Here is the cup of My Blood."

I could barely make out His form in the brightness of His Father's glory. With His arm still outstretched, He took another step toward the Throne of God, the Seat of Mercy, preparing to give the cup to His Father.

"This is for You, Father. I did it for You, just as You asked Me to."

He lifted the cup, now with both hands, to His Father. The angels could barely contain their suspense. They moved more noticeably now, as the Son continued to speak.

"I love You, My Father. This cup, with all it contains, with all it has accomplished, is Yours."

There was a deep groan from the very depth, the very heart of the Light, as Father stood to His feet. Through the brilliance of His splendor, I could barely make out the pale silhouettes of Father and Son falling toward each other, grasping one another with an embrace that has no words to describe.

The cup of Blood fell from His hand, splattering both Father and Son with the Blood that ever liveth. The force of their embrace knocked the cup directly on the Throne, the ultimate Mercy Seat, as Father pulled His Son forward to Himself, still locked in loving embrace.

"Sit here, O Son of My love. Sit here with Me, right next to Me."

Songs of triumph and victory filled Heaven as the angels sang the songs only they could sing, in languages only they could understand.

"What You have done, You have done once and for all time. You will never leave My Presence again. Come, sit here with Me, forever."

The falling cup shattered against the Mercy Seat, sending the Blood in every direction. It covered the Mercy Seat and the poles that lay at its feet in this dimension and the Blood covered the throne in the dimension of eternity. It splattered against its badger skin walls and fell to the ground in front of the torn veil in this dimension, to just in front of the Mercy Seat. The splattered Blood made an eternal pathway from the place of my humanity to His Presence. It splashed onto the cherubim that stood guard, sending them into a crescendo of worship that opened the heavens and invited a myriad of angels to sing the ultimate intention of the Lord:

Chapter Seventeen

"The kingdoms of this world have become the kingdoms of our Lord and of His Christ!"

Then nature itself responded. From the distant mountains, somewhere between eternity and time, came a rumbling, a clapping like the most awful thunderbolt you have ever heard, and a rift between dimensions opened in glorious splendor. Instantly, blackened clouds rolled down the mountainside as though hungrily looking for prey. Lightning opened the sky as Heaven itself was split open from side to side. Another rampaging, thunderous roar exploded from the mountain, and the voice of God Himself could be heard pouring from eternity, proclaiming from one side of the universe to another, "I, Myself, have brought My deliverance. My right hand, and My holy arm have gotten for Me the victory!"

His thundering words blazed through eternity, breaking into time and space, in and out and through every epoch of every time the earth had or will experience, vaporizing every obstacle as though it were less than nothing. It searched out every darkness and every evil. It ravaged every sickness and destroyed every bondage. His voice crushed every lie and shattered every tormenting word spewed from the mouth of hell itself. It pulverized every lofty human arrogance and finally swallowed up death itself. Then it spewed satan's awful intention into the lake of fire that will burn forever and ever.

"The cup of My Blood! The cup of My Blood!" the sweet voice of the Son echoed through the ages and into Heaven itself as His Father gathered His only Begotten forever to Himself, nevermore to be separated from His Son. "This cup is for You, Father!" But His Father barely heard those words as He declared to the universe, "My Beloved Son, My Beloved Son!"

Then with a crack of a mighty timber, the gates of hell tore open, and the redeemed of the Lord rose with joyous clamor. Union with God had been accomplished!

And then I looked, and the heavens opened, as the shattering of the cup had splintered the division between Heaven and earth, between where we had lived and where He has prepared us to live with Him. Then I heard the voice of many angels around the throne and the living creatures and the elders, and the number of them was myriads of myriads, and thousands of thousands, saying with a loud voice:

"Worthy is the Lamb that was slain to receive power and riches and wisdom and might and honor and glory and blessing."

And Heaven and earth united in a moment that transcended eternity. The groaning of the earth, of things created on our side, joined with every living thing on the other side. The sound of that from Heaven could not be distinguished from the sound of that which rose from every created thing on earth. I mean, I could never have imagined anything like it, as everything that is in Heaven and on the earth and under the earth and on the sea, and all things in them, cried out with deafening worship,

"To Him who sits on the throne, and to the Lamb, be blessing and honor and glory and dominion forever and ever."

And still other angels appeared from the heavens, shouting,

"Worthy are You to take the book, and to break its seals; for You were slain and did purchase for God with Your blood men from every tribe and tongue and people and nation.

"And You have made them to be a kingdom and priests to our God, and they will reign upon the earth."

Then I saw the Lord, seated in union with His Father upon the Mercy Seat. His form was now clearly visible as the hosts of

Chapter Seventeen

Heaven worshiped, sang, shouted, danced, and worshiped some more.

"Yes!" I shouted with the angels. "It is finished! It truly is finished!

I was overwhelmed with the wonder of all that was happening in this realm of eternity. I was shocked at the reality of such joyful confidence and complete commitment the Lord has toward us. Oh, how foolish the guilt! How foolish the fear! How foolish the time I have wasted, the things I have believed! I am loved! I am loved! His Blood calls to humanity, "Come on in!" The Son calls to humanity, "Come on in! I have prepared a seat for you next to your Father and Mine, your God and Mine." The Father Himself, with hilarious joy, calls humanity, "Come on in! Take a seat and watch Me make your enemies a hassock for your feet!"

Nonetheless, I was happy to be peeking through the veil from the Holy Place, hiding as best I could from this supernatural opus of total rapture toward the One who sits on the throne. As much as I wanted to be part of this, dare I believe? Could He have been referring to me as well? Dare I go in knowing what I know about myself, with all that still troubles me?

The Lord saw me looking through the veil and motioned for me to come in. It was quite unbelievable that He would even notice me in the midst of such deafening worship.

But I wondered, *Dare I believe?*

The Blood splattered on the floor glistened as brightly as the light that pulsated from between the cherubim. Could it be?

Was He calling out to me? It did not take long for everything inside of me to cry out to Him. I wanted to run to Him. Almost against my will I inched ever so slowly through the veil. "This is just a dream or vision," I tried to reassure myself. "I have already been through this." But I am afraid I was not too convincing. Without warning I let go of the veil. There I stood, just inside the Most Holy Place, where He is Lord, where His will supersedes my will, where I relinquish my arguments and trust Him. But I was overcome with the knowledge that He had prepared a place for me as well on the very seat that He Himself sat with His Father.

In the splendor of that wonderful moment, all my fears and my meager human frailty seemed to be nothing against the power of the love of the Lord calling me to Himself. I was about to run to Him. My flesh screamed as it began to realize it was about to lose its favored position as counselor and confidant of all my decisions.

Then, I finally did it. I dropped everything I could and ran with all I was worth. Yes, I tripped over my own personal clutter. I clanged with all the fleshly stuff still tightly fastened to me. I knew I was in desperate need; I knew I looked rather unkempt to myself, but I also knew He was calling to me. So I ran to Him, to His open arms, to His open heart, to His mercy, and to His forgiveness. I ran to His power to deliver and His desire for the likes of someone like me. I ran to His smiling face that seemed to hold as much anticipation as a mother watching her child take his first steps.

The clutter and clang of all I still dragged with me was drowned by the glory of angelic worship. The blinding light of His Manifest Presence seemed to make my humanity disappear as I approached Him who dwells in unapproachable Light. In a moment I was with Him or in Him or beside Him, in this dimension or the other, I did not know and I did not really care what correct doctrinal spin to give it. I knew I was in my body, but I also knew I was in Him, really in Him. Oh, but it did not matter if I could explain it. I would leave that part to those who try to figure out events like this. I would simply enjoy Him. All I did know was that I was completely consumed by Him.

"My yoke is easy," He whispered to me, "and My burden is light."

I held Him and I held Him and I held Him.

"Let My Blood cover you until My power delivers you."

He held me and He held me and He held me.

"I will put all your enemies exactly where they belong," the Lord spoke with eternal resolve, "right under your feet."

I found myself whispering softly to Him as He gathered me to Himself, "Yes, yes, yes, Lord. Thy Kingdom come. Thy will be done on earth as it is in Heaven. Thy Kingdom come in me, in my heart. Thy will be done in me, on earth, exactly as You have dreamed it for me in Heaven. Yes, yes, Lord. Yes, Lord."

Chapter Eighteen

J sat there on the Mercy Seat for the longest time, enjoying His Presence, but sorry that this was only a vision of what had already occurred in eternity. I knew that any moment He would awaken me or do whatever it was He did to take us back to where we had begun this side trip. The Lord had used these wonderful adventures to teach me some of the most incredible things, but this was truly the most incredible of them all.

"Thank You, Lord," I ventured to say to Him. "This is so overwhelming, so wonderful."

I hesitated to tell Him how I felt, but I had new confidence to talk to Him as the true Friend that He had become. "I do not want to go back," I said rather sheepishly, "but I guess we have to."

The Lord turned to me with an inquisitive look on His face.

"Why would you want to go back? If I were you, I would want to stay right here."

"Well, I do want to stay here, Lord. But I thought we always returned from these adventures once You had taught me everything I needed to see."

My words drifted into silence with the realization that He had somehow brought my reality into

His reality. Somehow, dimension had converged upon dimension and this was reality. This was not just a side trip. I actually was here in the midst of all the worshiping angelic hosts and in the Presence of the Father Himself!

"Lord, how did this happen?" I stammered. "I do not understand." I stood to look around the throne.

"I do not remember seeing all this within the veil. I do not remember seeing or hearing the angels. The cherubim were gold statues; now they are real. The Mercy Seat had only a light on it, and now the Father sits there. It was so quiet before, just You and I sitting there on the Mercy Seat. Now I can see and hear all this wonderful heavenly activity."

The Lord smiled gently, as usual.

"Yes, we were on the Mercy Seat, but this side trip opened your spiritual eyes to see things that you could not see before. Everything you see here now is as it was before. Now, however, you have eyes to see so much more of the things that were here all along.

"And there is much more for you to see and experience beyond the veil, beyond your fleshly self with all its demands and earthbound requirements.

"Life will never be the same. I will teach you things you thought you knew and show you things you were sure you understood. In many ways, your life will be turned upside down, or, more accurately, right side up. For as the doctrines and traditions of men are challenged by truth, you will discover the true freedom of Christ and understand the bondage you had been under for so many years."

I could not help but to be a bit uncertain as I heard these words. "But, Lord," I began, "people are always afraid of talk like that. They never are sure what they will get into if they hear the voice of the Lord for themselves. I have heard of some pretty strange things they claim You have said to them. Some say You are from Mars; some hear stones talking to them; some expect to see their dogs in Heaven."

"Yes, yes," the Lord stopped me with a smile, "I have some stories too."

"I bet You do," I returned the smile. "I guess that is why they say you can never count on your own interpretation of Scripture in your search for truth."

"That is easy to understand," the Lord countered. "They really are not so concerned about error. They do not want you to listen for yourself because they just want you to believe their interpretation of the Scripture. Some do not trust the Holy Spirit to lead their flocks into truth, so they attempt to prohibit them from listening to the Lord."

"But people do get into some awfully weird things in the name of Christianity," I protested to the Lord. I couldn't believe I was defending these guys.

"It is true that people get into things that are far from accurate. But how does that justify preventing the free, uninhibited seeking of the Lord in all His wonder and glory? Just because some miss the mark, the entire Church is punished? If the truth really be told, people still end up in error even with so many restrictions in place."

"But Lord, I want to be certain, Lord, that everything I hear and everything I do is absolutely scriptural, absolutely accurate."

"That is a noble statement, truly an admirable goal. But if you are so committed to that goal, why do you entrust your future to someone else? Why do you entrust your knowledge of the Lord and your love relationship to Him to anyone else but the Lover of your soul?

"Look, I am totally trustworthy. You can trust what I say. I do not violate my own Word," the Lord said with resolution. "Everything I say, everything I do, is according to the Word. You must remember, I AM the Word. The actual writing of it was an attempt to describe the nearly indescribable. I cannot do anything that will violate Myself and who I represent."

I already knew that, but somehow it was reassuring to hear that from Him. Still, there seemed to be something more He was not telling me, so I just waited.

He finally turned to me with a twinkle in His eyes. "However," He began.

I knew it! There was more, and I was about to hear it.

"However," the Lord began again, "although I can never violate My Word, I will always violate what men think My Word says. There is a big difference." Here the Lord paused with a smile. He shook His head as He continued, "Man will create doctrine out of the genuine conviction that he has properly understood and interpreted the Word. But when someone disagrees with what they determined is truth, that person is accused of heresy. Even more perplexing is when I do something that violates their doctrine. How quick they are to attribute My work to the flesh or satan! It is as though protecting their belief system is more important than the reality of My Presence.

"You must remember, although many want to experience God, that experience will not often fit within the context of what they have always believed. Your experience is not with a doctrine; it is with a person."

"It is the sheer arrogance of humanity that can believe that man has unraveled the mysteries of an eternal God and the complexities of His infinite love and mercies.

"We have existed from eternity past and We will exist for eternity future. Far after time has ceased, We will still be as though We have just begun.

"Mere mortal man believes that he has so understood My majesty and My multi-dimensional Being that he can judge another's salvation using his own textbook as his plumb line. These folk search the Scriptures for truth, and they miss Me as they intricately examine the robe that I wear on My back."

I just shook my head in wonder. "I do not remember all this in the Book," I said to myself. "I learned what is right and what is wrong reading the Book, but never all of this."

As I spoke, the Lord pulled out a copy of the Book. It was a small copy. The cover, a deep burgundy leather, was slightly tattered. The pages were frayed slightly on the edges, and the black ribbon to mark the pages was seriously worn. It looked strangely like the one I kept on the nightstand next to my bed.

"You have been reading this for years."

"Yes, I have, Lord."

"But it brought you more frustration than peace."

I was so embarrassed, but He was right. "Yes, Lord, it has brought me a fair amount of frustration."

"Do you understand why it so unsettled you as you read?"

"Well, I guess it was because I could never do what it said for me to do. It made it so difficult to read sometimes."

"Ah," He interrupted me. "That is the problem. It is always the problem."

"Reading the Book is a problem?"

"Reading the Book is not a problem. Reading it alone with only the five senses to help you understand is a big, big problem."

He opened the Book randomly as He spoke. Then He held it up, high over His head.

"Look, tell Me what you see."

"Look where?"

"Look into the Book."

"I cannot read it when You hold it up like that."

"Will you just look up into the Book?"

I moved closer to the Lord so I could see more clearly. I could feel His warmth as I nudged closer. *Wow,* I thought, *this is quite a perk. I get to be closer to Him as I read.*

Then I lifted my head and peered into the Book. I wondered what was on the page that was so important. I had thought that He opened the Book randomly. I squinted as I looked, assuming that He wanted me to read something special there.

I held my breath in amazement as I discovered what the Lord wanted me to see. For as I looked up at the Book, with Him holding it, I realized that I was not looking at the Book, but I was looking *through* the Book. In fact, it was not a book at all. It was, or seemed to be, a window.

The most indescribable things were in that window.

"Lord, what is this? I thought this was my copy of the Book, but this is some kind of special…"

Chapter Eighteen

"There is nothing special about this Book, except that I am holding it and directing your view."

"You mean all this is not really there? It is not real?"

"Oh, it is certainly real enough, but it is not visible to the natural dimension. It is not detectable to the five senses."

"Oh, my Lord, this is unbelievable. This is so awesome! How did You do this?"

"When you read with Me close, I direct the eyes of your spirit and lift your heart to a place of revelation and wisdom."

"But this is my Book. I have never seen any of this before."

"It is there when you want to see it."

As I gazed through this open window, I saw the wonders of eternity itself. I saw His love intricately woven through everything that lived. His Life grew out of every word that proceeded from His mouth. His Spirit flowed from His heart to the hearts of uncountable millions. His mercy and grace sang "Come" and His Blood covered everyone who called upon Him as they ventured nearer to His throne. He reached out His hand, inscribing His laws forever on willing and hungry hearts while all the angels sang of His power and fell prostrate before Him. His joy bubbled from the lives of children and adults alike as darkness and crying fled at the sound of His voice.

"This is beyond description." I shook my head in stunned disbelief. "How does one talk about this?" I asked the Lord.

"You don't, mostly." The Lord responded with quiet joy, His eyes shining with satisfaction to see how I had responded to the wonders of His Kingdom.

"This is not something that can be understood by the senses of the natural dimension. This must be experienced spirit to Spirit."

I am sorry to say that I did not quite get it, so He went on.

"The written Word is not a textbook. It is not a list of what is necessary to reserve a place in Heaven. It is not a neatly defined protocol of religious activity. The Word is a window through which you may see and understand the dimension of the eternal. It is how you are able to discover the boundless wonder and mystery of an eternal God who is far bigger and far more majestic than man can comprehend."

I must have looked a little distraught at the power of His words to me. They went deep into my spirit and challenged me to respond to His voice as He spoke so gently to my inner being. The Lord turned and spoke to me with a reassuring voice.

"But for you, My child, life is really just beginning. Although you have believed for many years, you are now free to live and experience everything your heart desired and your spirit craved. For you will see the King in all His glory and be taught by His Spirit. You will increase in compassion and love for all men as you increase in knowledge. For some have forgotten My heart's cry for Israel: 'Jerusalem, Jerusalem, city that kills the prophets and stones those who are sent to her! How often I wanted to gather your children together, the way a hen gathers her chicks under her wings, and you were unwilling.'"

He paused for a moment, holding back a tear before He continued.

"You will surely, easily recognize the ones I have personally taught by the genuine love they have for one another and for the love and compassion they show to the world around them.

You cannot separate true spiritual knowledge from who I AM, who I have always been. With true spiritual knowledge comes love, devotion, patience, mercy, kindness, forgiveness, and so much more that demonstrates to the world that I live within My own people.

"Genuine faith and love will send you to the hungry, the poor, the sick, and the lonely. As you learn of Me, allowing Me total reign in your life, I will take you places that few would go apart from Me. For you will learn and carry, as your burden, true love for all humanity that I have.

"It is a love that blesses and does not curse.

"It is a love that gathers and does not scatter.

"It is a love that forgives and never holds retribution in its heart.

"It is a love that covers and heals.

"It is a love that cannot be imitated.

"It is a love that cannot be taken away, for it endures forever and grows stronger and stronger with each passing day until at last you cry out with joy and liberty, 'It is no longer I who live, but it is Christ who lives in me, and the life I am leading, I am leading by the faith of the Son of God who loved me and gave Himself for me.' "

This was so incredible. My heart raced with anticipation of all He had said to me. This is what I had yearned for and desired for so long. Now, it seemed as though it was all within the possibilities of His love.

I wanted to ask more questions, but the Lord did not allow me to even try.

"No more questions now. Be at rest, My son, and be encouraged. The greatest adventure of your life is just beginning. You have only entered the doorway."

Well, I knew that was true. Just one look around the Most Holy Place proved that. This is undoubtedly the most amazing thing I have ever seen.

The Lord turned to me. "You are impressed with this? Wait until you see all this descending into the hearts of men and women around the world. That is a sight to behold.

"You will soon discover the life and the splendor that union produces.

"Son, you are done working for yourself. Now you really do belong to Me, not just by doctrine, but in reality. And what you have always hoped for will come to pass. We have much to do together."

I did not want do anything or to go anywhere or see anything else right now. I was quite content to stay just where I was. I had no interest in further adventures. I was happy to be in His Presence, safe and secure.

"You will not leave this place ever again. But there is much more, My son."

The Lord spoke with such thrilling encouragement. But I was tired of working. If I did anything else or went anywhere else, He would have to not only lead me, He would have to go with me.

"I will do more than go with you, My son. You will never work apart from Me. We will work in harmony in all we accomplish. Everything you do, you will do in Me. Everything I will do, I will do through you."

Chapter Eighteen

"Sounds like synchronized swimming to me."

"No, this is not synchronized swimming," the Lord laughed out loud, shaking His head. "You are just beginning to discover the essence of union and the reality of true destiny."

I stared at Him there for a moment in sheer wonder that God might enjoy being with me as I enjoyed being with Him. More than that, He wanted to actually live and love and heal the nations through me! Incredible!

The Lord watched me and waited for me to recover from that most wonderful revelation. "Religion is satisfied for you to look like Me and act like Me. The outer appearance is everything to the system. But from the beginning, it was not to be this way. From the beginning, there would be a people who would yield to Me, trust Me, love Me. There would be a people through whom I would show Myself to the world, pouring out My love, My compassion, and My desire."

"Yes, Lord, this is what I want, what I live for. I want to please You, to give myself to You."

"And so you shall, so you shall."

Chapter Nineteen

Well. One would certainly think that once a person had responded to the wooing love of the Lord to join Him on the seat of ultimate mercy, it would be the end of the journey, or at least the end of the search. But it was only the end of the beginning, for there was so much more.

Now, however, the difference was huge indeed.

For now, the search was with the Lord and not for the Lord.

Destiny was in process and not in limbo.

Now one could walk with the Lord in the cool of the morning instead of wondering where He was in the gloom of night.

For the Lord, whom I serve, had suddenly come to His temple, my heart, the holiest place of all.

It was here that I discovered that I really love doing the work of the Lord. The problem before was simply that I was doing the work. It was a remarkable revelation. He never called me to work for Him or to act like Him; He called me to simply say "yes" to Him so that He could freely live His life through me.

But as usual, I got it all messed up.

Secretly, I really did not want to say "yes" to Him, so I devised all kinds of ways to appear as though He was living His life through me when really I was only pretending to be yielding to Him.

I knew His voice; I just chose to ignore it. I preferred a shallow life as opposed to responding to His leading deep in my heart. In those days, I was the one in charge of things. Now, by His mercy, He is the One in charge. He is the One who makes the decisions.

Things are much different in this dimension, this Most Holy Place, where I voluntarily lay down my will for His. In this dimension, I live in the conscious decision that I have once and for all yielded myself to Him.

But in the Holy Place, the dimension fraught with humanity in all its idiosyncrasies and selfishness, every decision turns into a major argument between the flesh, the Spirit of the Lord, and sometimes the enemy. That kind of arduous struggle always wears me down. It saps me of strength and time. It clouds my spirit and makes it difficult for me to hear Him say anything. I am most happy to say that those days are mostly behind me.

I am looking forward to saying "yes" to Him regularly, daily, even moment by moment. In the long run, it is certainly much easier, much more peaceful and fulfilling.

Living in the "yes" of God changes my responses to life's circumstances and the leading of the Lord. I have already determined that I have nothing to lose and absolutely nothing to argue about. Now, whenever I come to one of those frightening walls I do not want to face, I simply remind myself that I have already made the decision to agree with Him, no matter what.

Chapter Nineteen

I do not really know what life will hold beyond my fleshly humanity, beyond the veil of human control. However, I am certain that His plan for me, His desire for me, can only be far better than my own meager attempts for meaning and ultimate fulfillment.

The Lord gently broke into my thoughts. Suddenly all the sounds and activity of heavenly worship rushed into my spirit. He had my full attention.

"You should not be surprised to feel things more strongly than you have ever felt them before. Now you will begin to feel what Father feels. Everything Father feels, He feels passionately and completely. He does not fear emotion, for it is the overflow of His total commitment and determination to draw humanity to Himself. It will certainly be a new experience for you, and it may be a little unnerving."

No sooner had He spoken than I caught a glimpse of the Light that had escaped the Most Holy Place when the Lord first entered the torn veil. It continued its boundless journey through the ages, touching every time and every nation. It was not a haphazard flash of light, but a calculated, methodical search for everyone who ever lived. Upon each one, the Light of His Glory rested, urging, nudging, calling, drawing each person to Him who sits on the throne.

I sat in awe of the Light's gentle determination to shine in the heart of every person, revealing the love and forgiving power of the Christ of God.

I found myself captivated with its work. I watched as the Light approached each heart. I found myself praying on the breast of Father on behalf of these people I did not even know. I held my breath in anticipation as His love poured into the hearts of folks in every epoch.

I prayed fervently as I saw so many turn in rejection of the Son. I wept as I witnessed the Light shut out of so many lives. My tears of intercession turned the Lord back to those who had rejected Him only moments before. Some melted before Him on repeated attempts to break into their lives, but many, so many did not. I turned my body on the Mercy Seat to somehow get closer to Father as I prayed. As I did, I realized that I was not the only one who was in fervent intercession. In fact, the prayers I prayed flowed out of the endless compassion of the One who gave Himself for those who were now deciding to reject His eternal love and compassionate mercy.

I wept as He wept.

I prayed as He prayed.

I was overwhelmed with love as He was.

Every sound we made, every cry we cried, moved the heart of Father. He did not need to hear words, for every groan from the deepest place in our hearts reverberated with the mercy, the grace, and the desire of the Father.

Words only hinder the power of His Spirit, cluttering the air with human desire and fleshly, mental gymnastics in our frail, earthly attempts to solve each one's dilemma as they, too, wrestled with their own humanity. No, words were not at the heart of genuine intercessory prayer. I watched the Lord and yielded to Him. I understood that He needed me only to agree with what He already knew needed to be done. My participation caused eternity itself, and the plan He had determined, to flow effortlessly into the dimension of the five senses. It is here that

Chapter Nineteen

His work is accomplished. It is here that His love is displayed through simple folks like you and I who live only to please Him and to be found in the center of His marvelous activity on this planet.

Eternity itself flowed into time and space as I found myself groaning in prayer with an intensity I never before imagined.

Never before had I increased in faith as I lived in intercessory communion with my Lord.

Never had I spoken less and said more.

Never had I seen more and understood less.

Never had I been so content.

Never had the joy of the Lord been so wonderful as I agreed with the Lord, watching angels pour into the dimension of mere mortal man, coming to the aid of flesh and blood.

The activity was beyond description.

The determination was beyond explanation.

The love was beyond comprehension.

Some responded in a moment of time. Others allowed the Light of His glory a bit of room within them, preserving the hope that His love would ultimately overpower the "no" that resides within all of us. One thing was certain—salvation began to work in the heart of man the moment he began to search for Him who is Truth. And salvation continued to work in the heart of a man long after he determined in his heart of hearts to yield to His love, His purpose, and His destiny.

Countless myriads responded to Him as He cried throughout the ages, throughout all time, "Eye has not seen, ear has not heard, neither has it entered it into the hearts of man all that I have prepared for those who love Me."

Many believed. Many came to Him. Many felt the wonder of His Presence as His Light shone brightly into their hearts, warming them to the depths of their beings.

The more people melted in His Presence, the more faith rose within me. I found myself pressing against Him with anticipation of what would happen next in response to this mortal man's prayer.

Chapter Twenty

As I leaned against Him there on the Mercy Seat praying as I was inspired by my Lord, I heard the voice of the Father.

"Go." It was all He said.

"Go," He repeated.

Was He talking to me? I did not want to go anywhere. I was content to stay where I was, nestled close to Him in prayer. Surely He was talking to someone else, someone who did not pray as I was praying. Surely He needed me to pray. He needed me to break into eternity and rend the heavens so that which was eternal could flow into time and space. Surely...

"Go."

Surely He meant for me to stay where...

"Go."

But who would pray? Who would stand in the gap for those who needed Him and needed to be...

"Go."

"Okay! I will go! I will go. Yes, I will do what You want me to do." I turned to the Lord Jesus, who sat with me as I prayed. "I will go, but I do not want to leave the Presence of the Father."

The Lord smiled a surprised-looking smile. "I did not hear Him say you would leave His Presence. He simply said to go." Seeing my perplexed look, He continued, "Do you think I was alone as I walked among men? Do you think I was alone as I ministered to the masses and healed the broken of body and soul? Did you really think that 'go' meant that you would have to leave His Presence to do His will?"

"Well, I don't know. I mean, of course not. I would really go, I guess. But how would I do His bidding if I did not leave His Presence?"

The Lord just looked at me patiently without responding.

I stared back…rather vacantly, I might add. It is sort of an odd silence when the Lord is looking at you, waiting for an intelligent response.

But I am not really so dense. Finally it came to me. "I get it! I will go but never leave His Presence!"

The Lord smiled with relief.

"I get it. Saying 'yes' means I do what He wants. So I go where He is going so He can do what He wants to do through me."

"You did get it!" the Lord laughed.

"You never have to leave the Presence of the Father. Simply go where He is going and do what He is doing. You will change everything around you without even trying."

"Let's go!" I shouted, suddenly filled with a fresh sense of faith.

Once again, we were gone before I realized what was happening. I followed Him from place to place, from mountain to valley and back again to the mountain. I was doing things I never knew I could do. He took me to places where I never thought I would ever see Jesus going, and there I was with Him. Amazing.

"I should be afraid someone will see me here," I laughed to the Lord. "I could get into big trouble, You know. I might ruin my witness!"

We laughed together. I realized that the only witness I have is He that lives within me.

"Well, if anyone asks me what I was doing here, I will say that You sent me and that You came along." We laughed again.

"My, my, my, Lord!" I giggled uncontrollably. "What is happening to me?" Tears of joy streamed down our faces.

This "yes" of God was far from the predictable religious behavior I had been used to for so many years. This was far more exciting and far more rewarding. People were actually responding! There were no tricks, no gimmicks, no religious fads to lure a tired and bored humanity, a tired and bored church system. There were no little books scaring people into doing whatever you wanted them to do. These people were really falling in love with Jesus! They were actually following Him because they wanted to!

I struggled to speak through my laughter. "Oh, Lord, I cannot believe it." I had to wait for another attack of laughter to wear down before I could continue.

"I would normally have to spend hours coming up with spurious Bible studies to explain why most of what we did had no fruit. Oh...my...I cannot control this." My eyes were watering with joyful mirth. "Oh my, Lord. I am sorry. I guess this is not very funny." He did not give me an answer so I looked to where He was standing. When our eyes met, we both once again broke out into uncontrollable and most certainly non-religious laughter.

Again, I had to work to recover. "Lord," I finally was able to speak, "what would people say if they knew what we were laughing about? They would be so offended."

Giving me a deadpan look, the Lord said, "Many people would be offended if they saw Me laughing about anything."

"Lord, I cannot believe You said that!" We laughed together late into the night. I must have been dreaming, but I knew I was not. I was enjoying time with the One I loved.

Times were certainly different. How liberating to be able to respond to the Lord and not to man or his expectations of me. I was free to do only what He wanted. My future belonged to Him. My times were in His hands. My goal, my passion, my joy was now simply to say "yes" to Him every day.

Would I mess up again? Would I fall occasionally into sin? Unfortunately, but honestly, yes. But I am with Him on the Mercy Seat where mercy and grace run freely and forgiveness strengthens me to go on. The stench of sin wants me to carry guilt and live in depression, but I have experienced His love. I will not go back to guilt. I will not go back to shame. To be sure, each failure is a humbling experience. I realize how weak I am. I get frustrated, and I wonder how He can endure my weakness another minute, especially when it seems as though I fail again and again.

Chapter Twenty

But I know whom I have believed in and I am persuaded of His love. He is not only able, but He also wants to forgive me and empower me to go on. He wants to fulfill His destiny for me.

He knows I am just dust. I know I am just dust.

He knows the love He has for Me. I am discovering the love He has for me.

He knows what I can do. I am discovering what I can do.

He has dreamed a dream for me. I will, by the grace of God, fulfill the dream He has for me.

I am becoming more and more convinced that if God is for us, who can be against us?

Who will bring a charge against me? Who has the right, who has the authority, to separate me from my Lord? Who has the right to tell me I cannot be forgiven until I go through someone's concocted plan of religious gymnastics? Who has the right to stop me short of His glory?

For I am convinced that neither death, nor life, nor angels, nor principalities, nor things present, nor things to come, nor powers, nor height, nor depth, nor any other created thing, shall be able to separate us from the love of God, which is in Christ Jesus our Lord.

I am hidden in Christ, covered with His Blood, held by His love at the Mercy Seat of His throne. There He continuously loves me, forgives me, empowers me, and causes me to live in the "yes" of His purpose.

He has romanced me.

He holds me.

He keeps me.

I do not have to convince Him to love me or desire me or be patient with me. He is all over me with desire and love and patience.

This is certain: The Lord whom I have spent a lifetime romancing, was romancing me all along. The One I was trying to win had already been won, without any effort on my part.

It was true love from the very beginning.

It will be true love until my final breath.

Then, it will be true love for all eternity.

In Conclusion

J have spent my entire life trying to entice, to please, to romance, and to otherwise get the attention of my Lord. I have wanted Him more than any other thing on the planet. I have plotted, planned, worked, and studied to discover how I could convince Him to love me as I have loved Him.

Yes, I am just an ordinary person. I struggle. I fail. I hope.

I am very ordinary.

There is nothing about me that would cause anyone, let alone the God of creation, to take even a glance my way as He walked by. I have read the books of great men. I have heard the sermons of those who have studied Him. I have watched the gifted. I have imitated the holy. I have parroted the prayers of those who are supposed to know.

None of it worked.

I am hopelessly average.

No amount of reading or studying or plotting will ever change that. It makes me wonder why He would take a second look at me once I have gotten His attention. What will He see? What will impress Him? I ask as though I do not already know. But, to be honest, I know what He will see. He will see me.

That's all. Just me. He will see my failures, my weakness, my confusion—but mostly my weakness. He will see my struggle, my pain, my insecurity.

There are no eloquent words that can change that. After a lifetime of searching and struggling and anticipating, He will see only me.

So after all these years, after all this time and struggle, here we are, Lord. Face to face, Heart to heart, Love to love, Desire to desire, Passion to passion. Here I am. Incredible. I have been determined to make myself as lovable, attractive, obedient, and as good as possible hoping to somehow attract You, to somehow get Your attention even in the midst of this universe full of beautiful things and beautiful people. I have tried to stand out among such intense competition, among all those who clamor for Your attention.

I have fought and worried and connived all these years only to find—wonder of wonders—that He has been romancing me all along. This King of kings, this Lord of lords already loves me, already wants my friendship, already is determined to gather me to Himself in a union that cannot be described by mortal man.

The clamor of so many very important things He has to tend to has not diminished His desire for me. It has not diminished His passion for the likes of me. He wants me as I have wanted Him! Well. Now this is almost too much to take. After all, I am nothing, I have nothing, I can do nothing worthy of the Lord God Almighty. But that does not seem to matter to Him whose love is so magnetic, so convincing, so final.

For there is something else about me He will see. He will see my desire. He will see my love, my devotion, and, yes, He will see a heart that yearns for Him more than anything else on the planet. I know that my love is not perfect. I know that I struggle with things that may cause some to question my devotion. I understand that some require evidence that would cause me to appear as though I lack desire. I am certain that I would not measure up to the lists that certain men use to determine their definition of spirituality. But this is what I have. This is who I am. This is what He will see.

And He will be pleased. For He does not see as men see.

He does not judge as men do.

Hah! Here is the irony. I thought I was trying to get His attention all this time. I thought this burning desire for meaning and relevance within my heart was just there, almost by accident. But He wanted me so much that He put that burning desire for Him within me. So I would search out His love and His Presence. He has romanced me, indeed! It is, without question, the ultimate romance. For God so loved the world, me individually, me personally, that He planted Desire in my heart, that I may be overwhelmed with that desire to run after Him with everything that is within me.

Oh, when I think about how I almost quit. When I think about how I almost believed the lies that would have kept me away from Him. Thank God! He loves me, little ole me. He wants me. It does not matter what the religious right or the religious left may say. I am loved and there is nothing that can separate me from that love. Now that I have found Him whom my soul doth love, I will not run *to* Him; I will run *with* Him. I will not work *for* Him; I will work *with* Him. I will not worship to *get* His attention. I will worship because I *have* His all. I won't worship to *gain* His favor but because I *have* His favor. I know I am in the palm of His hand. I know He has my life under His control.

Therein does my search forever change. Therein does my heart rejoice and my spirit rest. I please Him. I just please Him. I know it sounds awfully strange, but I can get used to it. I please the Lord. I bring a smile to His face and a song to His heart. He wants to be with me. He wants to live within me.

Yes, yes, I know there are things within me that do not please Him but they do not please me either. He will set me free from them at the right time. I really do not think that these nagging weaknesses can dwell for very long with the Light of all the universe commanding ruling interest in my heart.

Once I walked in darkness, but now I walk in the Light of the world.

Once I had not received mercy, but now I have received mercy.

Once I tried to Romance the Divine, but now I have discovered that He has romanced me.

Once, I was content with the fleeting love of a system that could not really love at all.

But now, well, now I have found true love.

Other books by

by Don Nori

NO MORE SOUR GRAPES

Who among us wants our children to be free from the struggles we have had to bear? Who among us wants the lives of our children to be full of victory and love for their Lord? Who among us wants the hard-earned lessons from our lives given freely to our children? All these are not only possible, they are also God's will. You can be one of those who share the excitement and joy of seeing your children step into the destiny God has for them. If you answered "yes" to these questions, the pages of this book are full of hope and help for you and others just like you.
ISBN 0-7684-2037-7

THE HOPE OF THE NATION THAT PRAYS

The Hope of the Nation That Prays gives clear answers about God's love and His will for America. Will God answer our prayers? What prayers can we pray? What is God's will for America? What is God's will for me personally? Included are prayers for our country and for those we love, based upon scriptures from the Bible. Take a step back in time with prayers from historical figures who have experienced extraordinary answers to prayers in times of crisis. Featured, are prayers from such great leaders as George Washington, Martin Luther King, Jr., Abraham Lincoln, and many others.
ISBN 0-7684-3045-3

THE ANGEL AND THE JUDGMENT

Few understand the power of our judgments—or the aftermath of the words we speak in thoughtless, emotional pain. In this powerful story about a preacher and an angel, you'll see how the heavens respond and how the earth is changed by the words we utter in secret.
ISBN 1-56043-154-7

HIS MANIFEST PRESENCE

This is a passionate look at God's desire for a people with whom He can have intimate fellowship. Not simply a book on worship, it faces our triumphs as well as our sorrows in relation to God's plan for a dwelling place that is splendid in holiness and love.
ISBN 0-914903-48-9
Also available in Spanish.
ISBN 1-56043-079-6

SECRETS OF THE MOST HOLY PLACE

Here is a prophetic parable you will read again and again. The winds of God are blowing, drawing you to His Life within the Veil of the Most Holy Place. There you begin to see as you experience a depth of relationship your heart has yearned for. This book is a living, dynamic experience with God!
ISBN 1-56043-076-1

HOW TO FIND GOD'S LOVE

Here is a heartwarming story about three people who tell their stories of tragedy, fear, and disease, and how God showed them His love in a real way.
ISBN 0-914903-28-4
Also available in Spanish.
ISBN 1-56043-024-9

Available at your local Christian bookstore.

For more information and sample chapters, visit www.destinyimage.com

Additional copies of this book and other
book titles from DESTINY IMAGE are
available at your local bookstore.

For a complete list of our titles,
visit us at www.destinyimage.com
Send a request for a catalog to:

Destiny Image® Publishers, Inc.
P.O. Box 310
Shippensburg, PA 17257-0310

*"Speaking to the Purposes of God for This
Generation and for the Generations to Come"*